Paramount Gift Books

What the Quran Says About Allah

Prof. Muhammad Rafi

Paramount Books (Pvt) Ltd.
Karachi | Lahore | Islamabad | Hyderabad | Faisalabad | Peshawar | Abbotabad

What the Quran Says About Allah

by

Prof. Muhammad Rafi

First Edition 2014

Paramount Books (Pvt) Ltd.
152/O, Block-2, P.E.C.H.S., Karachi-75400, Pakistan
Tel: 34310030, Fax: 34553772, E-mail: paramount@cyber.net.pk
Website: www.paramountbooks.com.pk

ISBN: 978-969-637-024-6
Printed in Pakistan

INTRODUCTION

Mankind practices different religions. Some of them are Divinely revealed, while others are not. Man-made religions are an abomination before Allah and will never succeed in the long run. The Quran terms Islam as 'Deen' (way of leading life positively). It is not a religion in the sense we use the term. The Arabic word 'Islam' simply means submission and derives from a word meaning 'peace'. In a religious context, it means complete submission to the will of Allah. The directives and guidance of the Almighty are preserved for all times in the Quran which is the last and final of the revealed books. Muhammad ﷺ is the last Messenger of Allah on to whom the Quran was revealed.

Quran is the only source and religious book in the world in which Allah addresses mankind in the first person (We, Us, Our). It is a monograph that finds its way from the mind to the heart. As we proceed, we notice that this Book of Guidance leaves no lingering doubts in a sincere, truth seeking heart and mind. Allah Himself guarantees the truth of this Revelation, its explanation and its preservation; Quran is free of all contradictions.

Quran is a book of precepts, injunctions, admonition, commands, warnings and advice. It is not meant to provide shade to a bride leaving her home after her wedding. It is a book of guidance and prescriptions that will do no good if they are worn like a charm and applied in life.

The exalted Nabi Muhammadﷺ was asked about Allah. Allah responded in Quran in a very succinct yet comprehensive chapter This chapter is considered to be the essence of the Oneness, the unity and the root of monotheism.

112:1 SAY: "He is the One God" :112:2 "God the Eternal, the Uncaused Cause of All Being." 112:3 "He begets not, and neither is He begotten; 112:4 ("and there is nothing that could be compared with Him."

This booklet uses the term Allah instead of the commonly used term 'God' as the Quran also does so. The Quran helps us in understanding the infinite Might, Authority, Compassion, Mercy and Wisdom and countless other attributes of Allah . The only source of knowledge about Allah is only possible through the Divine Books revealed to the exalted Messengers (Anbiya Karam). The Quran points out that Allah alone is the Creator and He is self-existent as well as self-subsistent. He alone creates and determines all 'causes' and 'effects'. That is why we speak of Him as the Sustainer (Rabb) Who gives and holds life and death to His creations. All 'causes' have their beginning with Him, and all 'effects' find their ending in Him. He alone is the First and the Last, the Eternal, the Initiator and the Determiner. He neither begets nor was he begotten and nothing whatsoever is like Him.

We identify Allah through the variety and beauty of His creation and through His magnificent order and harmony in the universe. He makes Himself known to His conscious and obedient servants through the manifestations of His attributes. Believing in Allah leads to submission to His Guidance. Submission is a willing and intending obedience to Allah in all His Commands, Directives and Prohibitions. A true Muslim leads his life in accordance with these Divinely revealed values to attain peace and harmony in this world as well as the hereafter.

The Quran deals with the knowledge about Allah in a clear and novel way. As the sole and a prime source of learning the worldview of Islam, it applies the method of negation and affirmation in dealing with this important subject. Initially it negates, by means of convincing proofs and indications, the existence of false gods, because it is necessary first to negate all forms of pseudo-divinity and the worship of false gods. This is the first step on the path to unity. The Quran says:

21:24 Or have they taken for worship (other) gods besides Him? Say, "Bring your convincing proof: this is the Message of those with me and the Message of those before me." But most of them know not the Truth, and so turn away."

The next step is an affirmation of Divine Unity. No concept has ever occurred to man that is more productive of creative insight and more relevant to the various dimensions of human existence than the concept of Divine Unity. Using clear proofs the Quran shows the way to attain knowledge of Allah (59:22,23)

59:22 Allah is He, than whom there is no other god; - Who knows (all things) both secret and open; He, Most Gracious, Most Merciful.

59:23 Allah is He save whom there is no god: the Sovereign Supreme, the Holy, the One with whom all salvation rests, the Giver of Faith, the One who determines what is true and false, the Almighty, the One who subdues wrong and restores right, the One to whom all greatness belongs! Utterly remote is God, in His limitless glory, from anything to which men may ascribe a share in His divinity

Monotheism, the solitary rule of one 'Ilah' as presented in the Quran means one truth for all people- from the beginning of time; one Ilah, one mankind, one covenant.

GLOSSARY OF TERMS USED IN THE QURAN

1. Aaron/Harun/Haroon – Aaron was the elder brother of Moses. Both the brothers were Nabis (messengers)
2. Abraham/Ibrahim – Father of Ishmael and Isaac and grandfather of Jacob, was the first in the line of Anbiya (Messengers) sent to the people of Arabia
3. Adl – (Ain, Dal, Lam) means 'justice', but not merely the justice dispensed by a court of law; it covers justice in all spheres of life. Justice signifies the condition where every individual gets what is due to him. 'Due' means not only what is due to him economically but all the fundamental rights that belong to him by virtue of his being a human being.

4. Ajal – (alif jeem-lam) Allah never destroys a nation unless it brings destruction upon itself through its own-wrongdoing. The messengers of Allah came to them and were ridiculed and refuted. Refusal to change their ways resulted in those nations creating social ills and imbalance and they were ultimately destroyed. According to the above law, the time gap between an action and the manifestation of its result is a period of respite termed as 'Ajal'
5. Aleem – (ain-lam-meem) Ilm means knowledge, to know something positively, to recognize, to find reality to the extent of certainty, to feel, to find out definitely (Taj/ Moheet). One who knows these things in this process is called aalim (learned person), and its plural is aalimoon. Aalim (plural Ulama) is one whose knowledge is very deep,
6. Allah – (alif-lam-ha) This is the proper name of Allah (Al-llah), and all other names denote His various attributes. Ilah, by definition, is one: to whom someone looks for protection in bewilderment, by whose grandeur one gets dazed, whose overall sovereignty and ultimate authority is accepted, whose laws and commands are obeyed and followed, and who is at the highest pedestal and remains unseen (Taj). Keeping in view the above

attributes, the name 'Allah' as it appears in the Quran would mean a Being Who is supreme but remains hidden from human eyes; before whose dignity and grandeur human perceptions become dazed; whose sovereignty extends over the entire universe; whose obedience is mandatory. By accepting Him as 'Ilah', one must accept only His sovereignty and obey His laws. The human mind just cannot perceive Him in any shape or physical form nor can it explain Him. He is beyond human perceptions (6:104). Nothing is like Him (42:11). However, we can explain His attributes as mentioned in the Quran. To believe in Allah would, therefore, mean to acknowledge and accept His sovereignty with all His attributes, as mentioned in the Quran, in the most balanced and proportionate manner (17:110. It is, incorrect to say that the Allah of all religions is the same that Rama or Raheem is one and the same thing. The Holy Father of Christians, the Yahweh of Jews, the Ishwar or Parmatma of Hindus and Armazd of Zoroastrians are totally different from each other – as their attributes are different from those of Allah as defined in the Quran. He is above all such perceptions! He cannot be transformed out of stone or a log of wood. The correct concept of Allah can only be perceived by explaining His attributes as narrated in the Quran, since only the Quran is exalted from the interplay of human thought. It is because of this reason that the Quran does not accept the existence of Allahs, which various people, tribes, or religions have carved out of their own thoughts.

7. Anbiya – The plural form of nabi – see nabi.
8. Bani-Israel – (literally, 'the children of Israel'). Jacob (Yaqoob) was the grandson of Abraham. His title was Israel, which means 'man of Allah'. His descendants are known as the Bani-Israel His fourth son was Yahuda or Judea whose tribe settled in Palestine. From this reference, this tribe came to be known as Jew (Yahud) and the remaining tribes as the Bani-Israel
9. Deen – (dal-ya-noon) This word has been used in various forms and meanings, e.g. power, supremacy, ascendancy, sovereignty or lord ship, dominion, law, constitution, mastery, government, realm, decision, definite outcome, reward and punishment. On the other hand, this word is also used in the sense of obedience, submission and allegiance (Taj, Moheet). In the Holy

Quran this word is used in almost all the above meanings in as many as 79 verses. Ad-deen is to surrender before that supreme authority which provides nourishment to the entire universe and lays down the laws and the code (2:131–132). "The day of deen" is when no man has any power over another man and all the affairs of mankind. It would be decided according to the law of Allah. Verse (1:3) also gives reference to this day, period or stage of history when humankind would lead their lives according to the law of Allah. These laws of Allah in their final and complete form are given in the Quran, and are called ad-deen.

10. Eiman/Iman/momin/momineen – (alif-meem-noon). Amnun – Means peace, safety, a state of mind where one feels safe from fear or danger (2:24), safe, secure and at peace, peace of mind, to testify, the opposite of dishonesty To accept, to obey, to bow in obedience According to the Holy Quran, Eiman in the following five fundamental entities is demanded of one to become a Momin (2:177): Eiman in Allah means to have faith in His existence, to trust His every word, to depend upon the laws given by Him and declare that one would obey those laws.

To have faith in the law of Mukafat means to have firm conviction in that law and to have faith in the continuity of life after death. To have faith in Malaika means to believe that all heavenly forces operate in the universe to implement the tasks/programmes given to them by Allah, and that all heavenly forces have been made subservient to man. Eiman is usually translated in English as 'belief or 'faith', and 'faith in turn signifies blind acceptance without proof, argument, or reason. According to the Holy Quran, however, Eiman is not what has been described as above as believing. In fact, Eiman is synonymous with conviction and is based upon reason and knowledge. The Holy Quran does not recognize eiman as any belief that is divorced from reason and involves the blind acceptance of any postulate. Eiman, according to the Holy Quran, signifies the conviction that results from full mental acceptance and intellectual satisfaction. This kind of conviction gives one a feeling of amn - inner contentment and peace (Amn and Eiman have a common root)

11. Fitna – (fa-ta-noon) Fitna is used in the meaning of deviation or to go astray from the right path. In verse (22:11) it is used as opposite of khair (good). In verses (2:193,

8:39) it means to create chaos or disorder. Overall, in the Quran it is used in the meaning of deviation in reference to the hurdles put in the way of establishing the Quranic social order.

12. Gabriel – Stands for the angel Jibraeel
13. Ghafoor – (ghain-fa-ra) It is one of the attributes of Allah. It means the One Who provides Maghfirah. Maghfirah means protection and also forgiveness. Maghfirah also means to save a person from the punishment that is the outcome of his misdeeds (Mobeei). Maghfirah is usually translated as forgiveness.
14. Hajj – (ha-jeem-jeem) The annual pilgrimage to Makkah.
15. Hamd – (ha-meem-dal) It is the expression of the deep, intense feeling of appreciation invoked spontaneously when one sees an exceptionally beautiful and unique thing. The intention of uttering hamd i.e. to say al-Hamdulillah) is to acknowledge the greatness of whoever created the given object of admiration. 'Hamd Bari-e-Taala' means to praise Allah.
16. Haqq – It is a very comprehensive Quranic term. It is usually translated in English as truth or right. No belief or theory relating

to this world can be described as haqq unless its truth is established by a positive manifestation of its.

17. Haram – (ha-ra-meem) Haram is antonym of halal, which means forbiddenand also a place whose protection is necessary. Ashbur-ul-harum is the four months (Rajab, Zequad, Zul-Hajj and Muharram) wherein all fights were forbidden (Taj/Moheet). The authority to prohibit certain things (declare them haram) rests with Allah alone (7:32–33, 2:172–173). No one else is authorised to exercise this right.
18. Hijra – (ha-jeem-ra) Albajro means to leave something, to move from, to remove it, to separate from. Therefore, alHijra or hijra means to leave one area and move to another - in other words, to emigrate.
19. Iblees – (ba-lam-seen) Ab-lasdmeati & to feel dejected (Tbn-e-Faris). It also means to get dazed and The Holy Quran has presented Iblees as an embodiment of rebellion, disobedience, insubordination and revolt. He refused to obey Allah, took up a rebellious path and became among those who disobey (2:24), as opposed to Malaika, whose nature is total obedience without doubt to Allah's command (38:73). The Quran has termed Iblees and Satan

(SHAITAN) as the two faces of the same coin.

20. Injeel/the Gospel/the Bible – It is the name of the book revealed to Jesus.
21. Ishmael/Ismail – Ishmael was the elder of the two sons of Abraham, as mentioned in the Holy Quran.
22. Islam – (seen-lam-meem) This is the basic root for the most important words Islam and Muslim, necessitating, understanding its meaning fully and in depth. All the basic meanings have been taken from Lane, Taj. Islam means to bow in totality before the eternal laws given by Allah in letter and in spirit It is the only way of life which ensures reaching one's destiny (20:47) and anyone who follows a different path will be unable to bring about the expected results, and he ultimately will be doomed. Islam is that code of life, which has been revealed by Allah for mankind. There is no other code acceptable to Him. In Surah 3:82, the Quran says, "Do those people desire some different deen than the one ordained by Allah?" At yet another place, "If someone adopts a way other than this, it will not be acceptable and in the end he will be the loser (3:84)." This is the code, which was revealed to various anbiya from

time to time. This final and complete code of life was revealed to Rasool - Allah ﷺ and selected the whole of mankind. This code is called Al-Islam and the followers of the code are called Muslimeen (Muslims). A Muslim is he, who accepts the Holy Quran as the one and only complete and final code revealed by Allah for mankind.

23. Jacob/Yaqub/Yaqoob – Jacob was the son of Isaac, nephew of Ishma'el and grandson of Abraham. His title was Israel (man of Allah); that is why his generation is called the Bani-Israel the sons of Israel.
24. Jahannam – Generally, it means hell.
25. Jannah, Jannat – (jeem-noon-noon) It is usually translated as heaven or paradise.
26. Jesus – The name of Esa (Jesus) is mentioned 25 times and Maseeh, ibn-e-Maryam, 11 times in the Quran.
27. Kufr/kafir/kafireen – (kaf-f a-ra) Means to conceal, to hide, to cover. Keeping in view this meaning of hiding or covering, it was also used in the meaning of denial, refusal or rejection. Therefore, it was used in contrast to the concept of Eiman, i.e., one who denies the absolute truth as given in the Quran. In the Quran, the plural of kafir is given as kuffar, kafiroon or kafaratun. Then

there are various categories of kafireen e.g. those who not only refuse to accept but also hinder others from accepting it, sometimes by force.

28. Mary/Maryam – The literal meaning of this word is highly placed. The Holy Quran mentions Mary as the mother of Jesus (Esa) (3:45).
29. Moses – stands for the Messenger Musa.
30. Munafiqeen – (noon-fa-qaf) Munafiqeen (hypocrites): are those who in order to derive some benefits or personal gains join the Jamat-ul-momineen, but abandon them at the time of crisis after spreading disheartening rumours.
31. Mushrikeen – See shirk.
32. Muslim – The Arabic word 'Muslim' is derived from three letters (Seen, Laam, Meem). These letters give the word its basic concept and characteristic meaning, salama - means purified, perfect, complete in all respects; free of blemish. aslarna the one who submits, bows (i) in totality before the eternal Divine Laws in letter and spirit; (ii) and leads a balanced life, A person who has the above traits is a Muslim. A body or a group of such people is called Muslimeen, the followers of Islam. Hence, a Muslim

is one who accepts the Holy Quran as the complete and final Code of life revealed by the Sustainer of mankind.

33. Muttaqeen – (wao-qaf-ya) Muttaqee. a person who keeps away from things that are harmful to his personality and character, by adhering to the laws of Allah, thus rejecting a negative approach to life and accepting positive virtues and is conscious of his duties (See details under taqwa).
34. Firaun (Pharaoh) – It occurs in the Quran 74 times. The Pharaoh was the dynastic tide of Egyptian kings who ruled Egypt and were called Firaun.
35. Rabb, Rabubiyya – (ra-ba-ba) It is usually translated into English as the Lord, which does not convey the real meanings and significance of the Arabic word. It means one who provides nourishment, to process a thing with new additions, alterations or changes so that it should reach its Rabb means Nourisher, Cherisher and Sustaniner.
36. Shiateen – (plural of Shaitan).
37. Taqwa – (wao-qaf-ya) The common English equivalent, namely, piety, does not properly express the real meaning of the word. Taqwa would mean to obey and follow the laws of Allah. Surah Muhammad explains that

there are some people who follow their own ambitions, feelings or desires and others, who follow the laws of Allah the later category gets or attains taqwa (47:1 7) Therefore, muttaqeen are those people who keep away from things that are harmful to their personalities, by remaining in harmony with the laws of Allah, and thus get their personalities developed. Asad has used the term 'Allah-conscious' for Taqwa.

38. Wahi – (wao-ha-ya) - (Divine revelation) 'Wahi'is the Quranic term for divine message from Allah to His Messengers.
39. Zikr – (za-kaf-ra) To discuss, relate or mention The Divine laws are also called Zikrullah (39:23).

WHAT THE QURAN SAYS ABOUT ALLAH

All praise is due to Allah alone,
the Sustainer of all the worlds,
Most Gracious, Most Merciful
Master of the Day of Judgment, Thee
alone do we worship; and unto Thee
alone do we turn for aid. Guide us to
the straight path. The way of those
upon whom You have bestowed Your
blessings, not of those who have been
condemned (by You), nor of those
who go astray!

1:1-7

اَلْحَمْدُ لِلّٰهِ رَبِّ الْعٰلَمِيْنَ ۙ﴿۱﴾
الرَّحْمٰنِ الرَّحِيْمِ ۙ﴿۲﴾ مٰلِكِ
يَوْمِ الدِّيْنِ ؕ﴿۳﴾ اِيَّاكَ نَعْبُدُ وَ
اِيَّاكَ نَسْتَعِيْنُ ؕ﴿۴﴾ اِهْدِنَا الصِّرَاطَ
الْمُسْتَقِيْمَ ۙ﴿۵﴾ صِرَاطَ الَّذِيْنَ اَنْعَمْتَ
عَلَيْهِمْ ۙ﴿۶﴾ غَيْرِ الْمَغْضُوْبِ عَلَيْهِمْ
وَلَا الضَّآلِّيْنَ ﴿۷﴾ ع

The parable of misguided is that of people who kindle a fire: but as soon as it has illumined all around them, Allah takes away their light and leaves them in utter darkness, wherein they cannot see.

2:17

مَثَلُهُمْ كَمَثَلِ الَّذِى اسْتَوْقَدَ نَارًا ۚ

فَلَمَّآ اَضَآءَتْ مَا حَوْلَهٗ ذَهَبَ اللّٰهُ

بِنُوْرِهِمْ وَتَرَكَهُمْ فِىْ ظُلُمٰتٍ لَّا

يُبْصِرُوْنَ ﴿١٧﴾

O mankind! Obey your Sustainer (Rabb), Who has created you and those who lived before you, so that you might remain conscious of Him. Who has made the earth a resting-place for you and the sky a canopy, and has sent down water from the sky and thereby brought forth fruits for your sustenance: do not, then, claim that there is any power that could rival Allah, when you know the truth (that He is only One).

2:21, 22

يٰٓاَيُّهَا النَّاسُ اعۡبُدُوۡا رَبَّكُمُ
الَّذِىۡ خَلَقَكُمۡ وَالَّذِيۡنَ مِنۡ
قَبۡلِكُمۡ لَعَلَّكُمۡ تَتَّقُوۡنَ ۙ﴿۲۱﴾ الَّذِىۡ
جَعَلَ لَكُمُ الۡاَرۡضَ فِرٰشًا وَّالسَّمَآءَ
بِنَآءً ۖ وَّاَنۡزَلَ مِنَ السَّمَآءِ مَآءً
فَاَخۡرَجَ بِهٖ مِنَ الثَّمَرٰتِ رِزۡقًا لَّكُمۡ ۚ
فَلَا تَجۡعَلُوۡا لِلّٰهِ اَنۡدَادًا وَّاَنۡتُمۡ
تَعۡلَمُوۡنَ ﴿۲۲﴾

And your Allah is One Allah. There is no god but He, Most Gracious, Most Merciful.

2:163

وَإِلَـٰهُكُمْ إِلَـٰهٌ وَٰحِدٌ ۖ لَّآ إِلَـٰهَ إِلَّا هُوَ
ٱلرَّحْمَـٰنُ ٱلرَّحِيمُ ﴿١٦٣﴾

O You who have chosen to be graced with belief! Enjoy the clean, decent and aesthetically pleasing things that We have provided for all of you. And render thanks to Allah if it is Him you serve and obey.

2:172

يَاَيُّهَا الَّذِيْنَ اٰمَنُوْا كُلُوْا مِنْ
طَيِّبٰتِ مَا رَزَقْنٰكُمْ وَاشْكُرُوْا لِلّٰهِ
اِنْ كُنْتُمْ اِيَّاهُ تَعْبُدُوْنَ ﴿١٧٢﴾

When My servants ask you
(Muhammad) concerning Me, I am
indeed close (to them): I listen to the
prayer of every suppliant when he calls
on Me: Let them also, with a will,
Listen to My call, and believe in Me:
That they may walk in the right way.

2:186

وَ اِذَا سَاَلَكَ عِبَادِیْ عَنِّیْ فَاِنِّیْ
قَرِیْبٌ ؕ اُجِیْبُ دَعْوَةَ الدَّاعِ اِذَا
دَعَانِ ۙ فَلْیَسْتَجِیْبُوْا لِیْ وَلْیُؤْمِنُوْا
بِیْ لَعَلَّهُمْ یَرْشُدُوْنَ ﴿۱۸۶﴾

And whenever he is told, “Be conscious of Allah,” his false pride drives him into sin: wherefore hell will be his allotted portion–and how vile a resting-place! And there is the type of man who gives his life to earn the pleasure of Allah. And Allah is full of kindness to (His) devotees.

2:206, 207

وَ اِذَا قِیۡلَ لَہُ اتَّقِ اللّٰہَ اَخَذَتۡہُ الۡعِزَّۃُ
بِالۡاِثۡمِ فَحَسۡبُہٗ جَہَنَّمُ ؕ وَلَبِئۡسَ
الۡمِہَادُ ﴿۲۰۶﴾ وَ مِنَ النَّاسِ مَنۡ یَّشۡرِیۡ
نَفۡسَہُ ابۡتِغَآءَ مَرۡضَاتِ اللّٰہِ ؕ وَ اللّٰہُ
رَءُوۡفٌۢ بِالۡعِبَادِ ﴿۲۰۷﴾

Allah, the Wise and the Knowing, has said that He is the Sole Authority in the Universe and is Ever-living and Self-subsisting". "O Rasool: He has sent you this revelation based upon truth, which will validate the claims made in previous scriptures." Allah had previously sent the Torah and the Bible which contained guidance for mankind. Now, He has sent down this Book which distinguishes between right and wrong.". Those who will reject this Divine Code will suffer grievously according to Allah's Law of Mukaf'at. None can escape its grip. There is nothing in the universe which is hidden from Allah.

3:2–5

اللّٰهُ لَآ اِلٰهَ اِلَّا هُوَ ۙ
الْحَیُّ الْقَیُّوْمُ ؕ﴿۲﴾ نَزَّلَ
عَلَیْكَ الْكِتٰبَ بِالْحَقِّ مُصَدِّقًا
لِّمَا بَیْنَ یَدَیْهِ وَ اَنْزَلَ التَّوْرٰىةَ
وَ الْاِنْجِیْلَ ۙ﴿۳﴾ مِنْ قَبْلُ هُدًى لِّلنَّاسِ
وَ اَنْزَلَ الْفُرْقَانَ ؕ۬ اِنَّ الَّذِیْنَ كَفَرُوْا
بِاٰیٰتِ اللّٰهِ لَهُمْ عَذَابٌ شَدِیْدٌ ؕ وَ اللّٰهُ
عَزِیْزٌ ذُو انْتِقَامٍ ﴿۴﴾ اِنَّ اللّٰهَ لَا
یَخْفٰى عَلَیْهِ شَیْءٌ فِی الْاَرْضِ
وَ لَا فِی السَّمَآءِ ؕ﴿۵﴾

Alluring to man is the enjoyment of worldly desires through women, and children, and heaped-up treasures of gold and silver, and horses of high mark, and cattle, and lands. All this may be enjoyed in the life of this world–but the most beauteous of all goals is with Allah.

3:14

زُيِّنَ لِلنَّاسِ حُبُّ الشَّهَوٰتِ
مِنَ النِّسَآءِ وَالْبَنِيْنَ وَالْقَنٰطِيْرِ
الْمُقَنْطَرَةِ مِنَ الذَّهَبِ وَالْفِضَّةِ
وَالْخَيْلِ الْمُسَوَّمَةِ وَالْاَنْعٰمِ
وَالْحَرْثِ ؕ ذٰلِكَ مَتٰعُ الْحَيٰوةِ
الدُّنْيَا ۚ وَاللّٰهُ عِنْدَهٗ حُسْنُ
الْمَاٰبِ ﴿۱۴﴾

This is the true account . There is no authority but Allah. And Allah alone is Almighty, truly Wise. But if they turn back, Allah has full knowledge of those who do mischief.

3:62, 63

اِنَّ هٰذَا لَهُوَ الْقَصَصُ الْحَقُّ ۚ وَمَا
مِنْ اِلٰهٍ اِلَّا اللّٰهُ ؕ وَاِنَّ اللّٰهَ لَهُوَ الْعَزِيْزُ
الْحَكِيْمُ ﴿٦٢﴾ فَاِنْ تَوَلَّوْا فَاِنَّ اللّٰهَ عَلِيْمٌۢ
بِالْمُفْسِدِيْنَ ﴿٦٣﴾ ع

And how could you deny the truth when it is unto you that Allah's messages are being conveyed, and it is in your midst that His Messenger lives? But he who holds fast unto Allah has already been guided onto a straight way.

3:101

وَكَيْفَ تَكْفُرُوْنَ وَاَنْتُمْ تُتْلٰى
عَلَيْكُمْ اٰيٰتُ اللّٰهِ وَفِيْكُمْ رَسُوْلُهٗ ط
وَمَنْ يَّعْتَصِمْ بِاللّٰهِ فَقَدْ هُدِیَ اِلٰى
صِرٰطٍ مُّسْتَقِيْمٍ ﴿١٠١﴾ ع

Allah has indeed heard the saying of those who said, "Behold, Allah is poor while we are rich!" We shall record what they have said, as well as their slaying of prophets against all right, and We shall say (unto them on Judgment Day): "Taste suffering through fire."

3:181

لَقَدْ سَمِعَ اللّٰهُ قَوْلَ الَّذِيْنَ قَالُوْٓا
اِنَّ اللّٰهَ فَقِيْرٌ وَّ نَحْنُ اَغْنِيَآءُ ۘ
سَنَكْتُبُ مَا قَالُوْا وَ قَتْلَهُمُ الْاَنْبِيَآءَ
بِغَيْرِ حَقٍّ ۙ وَّ نَقُوْلُ ذُوْقُوْا عَذَابَ
الْحَرِيْقِ ﴿١٨١﴾

(and) who remember Allah when
they stand, and when they sit,
and when they lie down to sleep,
and (thus) reflect on the creation
of the heavens and the earth: "O
our Sustainer! Thou hast not created
(aught of) this without meaning
and purpose. Limitless art Thou in
Thy glory! Keep us safe, then, from
suffering through fire!

3:191

الَّذِيْنَ يَذْكُرُوْنَ اللّٰهَ قِيٰمًا وَّ قُعُوْدًا
وَّعَلٰى جُنُوْبِهِمْ وَيَتَفَكَّرُوْنَ فِيْ
خَلْقِ السَّمٰوٰتِ وَالْاَرْضِ ۚ رَبَّنَا مَا
خَلَقْتَ هٰذَا بَاطِلًا ۚ سُبْحٰنَكَ فَقِنَا
عَذَابَ النَّارِ ﴿١٩١﴾

Obey Allah and associate no partner with Him. Treat kindly your parents, relatives, the orphans, the needy and those who have been left alone in the society. Treat kindly your related neighbors, and unrelated neighbors, companions by your side, the wayfarer (you meet), and what your right hands possess: For Allah does not love those who are proud and boastful.

4:36

وَاعْبُدُوا اللّٰهَ وَلَا تُشْرِكُوْا
بِهٖ شَيْـًٔا وَّ بِالْوٰلِدَيْنِ اِحْسٰنًا
وَّبِذِی الْقُرْبٰی وَالْيَتٰمٰی
وَالْمَسٰكِيْنِ وَالْجَارِ ذِی الْقُرْبٰی
وَالْجَارِ الْجُنُبِ وَالصَّاحِبِ بِالْجَنْۢبِ
وَابْنِ السَّبِيْلِ ۙ وَمَا مَلَكَتْ
اَيْمٰنُكُمْ ؕ اِنَّ اللّٰهَ لَا يُحِبُّ مَنْ
كَانَ مُخْتَالًا فَخُوْرَا ۙ ﴿٣٦﴾

Allah - save whom there is no deity - will surely gather you all together on the Day of Resurrection, [the coming of] which is beyond all doubt: and whose word could be truer than Allah's?

4:87

اَللّٰهُ لَآ اِلٰهَ اِلَّا هُوَ ط لَيَجْمَعَنَّكُمْ اِلٰى
يَوْمِ الْقِيٰمَةِ لَا رَيْبَ فِيْهِ ط وَمَنْ
اَصْدَقُ مِنَ اللّٰهِ حَدِيْثًا ﴿۸۷﴾ ع

O People of the
Book! Commit no
excesses in your religion:
say nothing about Allah
except the truth. Christ Jesus
the son of Mary was (no more
than) a Messenger of Allah, the
fulfillment of His Word to Mary,
and a soul created by Him: so believe
in Allah and His Messengers, and say
not. 'Three' : desist: it will be better for
you: for Allah is one Allah. Glory be
to Him: Far removed it is from His
Supreme Majesty that He should
have a son. (far exalted is He) above
having a son. To Him belongs all
that is in the heavens and all
that is on earth; and none is
as worthy of trust as Allah

4:171

يٰۤاَهْلَ الْكِتٰبِ لَا تَغْلُوْا فِيْ
دِيْنِكُمْ وَلَا تَقُوْلُوْا عَلَى اللّٰهِ
اِلَّا الْحَقَّ ؕ اِنَّمَا الْمَسِيْحُ عِيْسَى
ابْنُ مَرْيَمَ رَسُوْلُ اللّٰهِ وَكَلِمَتُهٗ ۚ اَلْقٰهَاۤ
اِلٰى مَرْيَمَ وَرُوْحٌ مِّنْهُ ۫ فَاٰمِنُوْا بِاللّٰهِ
وَرُسُلِهٖ ۚ وَلَا تَقُوْلُوْا ثَلٰثَةٌ ؕ اِنْتَهُوْا
خَيْرًا لَّكُمْ ؕ اِنَّمَا اللّٰهُ اِلٰهٌ وَّاحِدٌ ؕ سُبْحٰنَهٗۤ
اَنْ يَّكُوْنَ لَهٗ وَلَدٌ ۘ لَهٗ مَا فِي السَّمٰوٰتِ
وَمَا فِي الْاَرْضِ ؕ وَكَفٰى بِاللّٰهِ
وَكِيْلًا ﴿۱۷۱﴾ ع

Will these people not turn towards Allah and seek His protection? They should remember that He alone is the Protector and Most Merciful.

5:74

اَفَلَا يَتُوْبُوْنَ اِلَى اللّٰهِ وَيَسْتَغْفِرُوْنَهٗ ؕ
وَاللّٰهُ غَفُوْرٌ رَّحِيْمٌ ﴿٧٤﴾

Say (O Muhammad): "What thing is most weighty in evidence?" Say: "(Allah) is witness between me and you; This Quran has been revealed to me by inspiration, that I may warn you and all whom it reaches. Can you possibly bear witness that besides Allah there is another Allah." Say: "No! I cannot bear witness!" Say: "But in truth He is the one Allah, and I disown what you associate with.

6:19

قُلْ اَیُّ شَیْءٍ اَکْبَرُ شَهٰدَةً ؕ قُلِ
اللّٰهُ ۙ شَهِیْدٌۢ بَیْنِیْ وَ بَیْنَكُمْ ۙ
وَ اُوْحِیَ اِلَیَّ هٰذَا الْقُرْاٰنُ لِاُنْذِرَكُمْ
بِهٖ وَمَنْۢ بَلَغَ ؕ اَىِٕنَّكُمْ لَتَشْهَدُوْنَ اَنَّ
مَعَ اللّٰهِ اٰلِهَةً اُخْرٰی ؕ قُلْ لَّاۤ اَشْهَدُ ۚ
قُلْ اِنَّمَا هُوَ اِلٰهٌ وَّاحِدٌ وَّ اِنَّنِیْ بَرِیْٓءٌ
مِّمَّا تُشْرِكُوْنَ ۟﴿۱۹﴾

Say to them (O Messenger): "If your faculties of sight, hearing and understanding are paralysed as a result of going against Allah's laws, is there anyone besides Allah who can restore them?" Reflect upon how We repeat Our basic teaching to impress its truth upon them but they turn away from it.

6:46

قُلْ اَرَءَيْتُمْ اِنْ اَخَذَ اللّٰهُ سَمْعَكُمْ

وَ اَبْصٰرَكُمْ وَ خَتَمَ عَلٰى قُلُوْبِكُمْ

مَّنْ اِلٰهٌ غَيْرُ اللّٰهِ يَاْتِيْكُمْ بِهٖ ؕ

اُنْظُرْ كَيْفَ نُصَرِّفُ الْاٰيٰتِ ثُمَّ هُمْ

يَصْدِفُوْنَ ﴿٤٦﴾

Do away not those who call on
their Sustainer (Rabb) morning and
evening, seeking His Grace. You are,
by no means, accountable for them,
and they are not accountable for you. If
you send them away, then you will be
among the unjust.

6:52

وَلَا تَطْرُدِ الَّذِيْنَ يَدْعُوْنَ رَبَّهُمْ
بِالْغَدٰوةِ وَ الْعَشِيِّ يُرِيْدُوْنَ
وَجْهَهٗ ؕ مَا عَلَيْكَ مِنْ حِسَابِهِمْ
مِّنْ شَيْءٍ وَّمَا مِنْ حِسَابِكَ عَلَيْهِمْ
مِّنْ شَيْءٍ فَتَطْرُدَهُمْ فَتَكُوْنَ مِنَ
الظّٰلِمِيْنَ ﴿٥٢﴾

And He alone holds sway over
His servants. And He sends forth
heavenly forces to watch over you
until, when death approaches any of
you, Our messengers cause him to die:
and they do not overlook (anyone).

6:61

وَ هُوَ الْقَاهِرُ فَوْقَ عِبَادِهٖ وَ يُرْسِلُ
عَلَيْكُمْ حَفَظَةً ؕ حَتّٰۤى اِذَا جَآءَ
اَحَدَكُمُ الْمَوْتُ تَوَفَّتْهُ رُسُلُنَا وَ
هُمْ لَا يُفَرِّطُوْنَ ﴿٦١﴾

And He is the One Who has created the heavens and earth with a definite purpose. Whenever He says "Be!" it is. His Word is the truth. And His will be the Dominion on the Day the Trumpet (of Resurrection) is blown. Knower of the Invisible and the Visible, for, He is the Wise, the Aware.

6:73

وَهُوَ الَّذِیْ خَلَقَ السَّمٰوٰتِ وَ
الْاَرْضَ بِالْحَقِّ ؕ وَیَوْمَ یَقُوْلُ
کُنْ فَیَکُوْنُ ۬ؕ قَوْلُهُ الْحَقُّ ؕ وَلَهُ
الْمُلْكُ یَوْمَ یُنْفَخُ فِی الصُّوْرِ ؕ عٰلِمُ
الْغَیْبِ وَ الشَّهَادَةِ ؕ وَهُوَ الْحَكِیْمُ
الْخَبِیْرُ ﴿۷۳﴾

This is Allah–your Nourisher (Rabb)–other than whom there is no authority, Creator of all things. Therefore, you should obey His–and only His–laws and remember that He is the Protector of all.

6:102

ذٰلِكُمُ اللّٰهُ رَبُّكُمْ ۚ لَآ اِلٰهَ اِلَّا هُوَ ۚ
خٰلِقُ كُلِّ شَيْءٍ فَاعْبُدُوْهُ ۚ وَهُوَ عَلٰى
كُلِّ شَيْءٍ وَّكِيْلٌ ﴿١٠٢﴾

No vision can grasp Him, but His grasp is over all vision: He is above all comprehension, yet is acquainted with all things.

6:103

لَا تُدۡرِكُهُ الۡاَبۡصٰرُ ۡ وَ هُوَ يُدۡرِكُ
الۡاَبۡصٰرَ ۚ وَ هُوَ اللَّطِيۡفُ الۡخَبِيۡرُ ﴿۱۰۳﴾

Your Nourisher (Rabb) has revealed the truth clearly. Whoever reflects on it, will do so to his own advantage. On the other hand, those who choose to remain blind to it, will do so to their own disadvantage. Remember I am not your keeper to force you to reflect.

6:104

قَدْ جَآءَكُمْ بَصَآئِرُ مِنْ رَّبِّكُمْ ۚ فَمَنْ
اَبْصَرَ فَلِنَفْسِهٖ ۚ وَ مَنْ عَمِیَ فَعَلَيْهَا ؕ
وَمَآ اَنَا عَلَيْكُمْ بِحَفِيْظٍ ﴿۱۰۴﴾

We have made the truth so clear in
diverse ways that those who reflect
on it, exclaim: "You have (O Rasool)
indeed separated the grain from the
chaff." In this way we have made it
manifest to a people who are disposed
to understand.

6:105

وَكَذٰلِكَ نُصَرِّفُ الْاٰيٰتِ وَلِيَقُوْلُوْا
دَرَسْتَ وَلِنُبَيِّنَهٗ لِقَوْمٍ يَّعْلَمُوْنَ ﴿١٠٥﴾

O Rasool (Messenger)you should follow that which has been revealed to you from Allah, other than whom there is no authority, and remain aloof from the Mushrikeen.

6:106

اِتَّبِعْ مَآ اُوْحِيَ اِلَيْكَ مِنْ رَّبِّكَ ۚ
لَآ اِلٰهَ اِلَّا هُوَ ۚ وَ اَعْرِضْ عَنِ
الْمُشْرِكِيْنَ ﴿١٠٦﴾

If it had been a part of Allah's plan that none should be a Mushrik, He would not have endowed human beings with free will. This is why we have not appointed you a guardian over them or responsible for their conduct.

6:107

وَلَوْ شَآءَ اللّٰهُ مَآ اَشْرَكُوْا ؕ وَمَا
جَعَلْنٰكَ عَلَيْهِمْ حَفِيْظًا ۚ وَمَآ اَنْتَ
عَلَيْهِمْ بِوَكِيْلٍ ﴿١٠٧﴾

The deities whom these people associate with Allah are no doubt false ones. This does not mean, however, that you may revile Allah in retaliation. They adhere to their beliefs because they seem fair to them. The nature of their deeds will become clear to them on the Day of Reckoning.

6:108

وَلَا تَسُبُّوا الَّذِيْنَ يَدْعُوْنَ مِنْ دُوْنِ
اللّٰهِ فَيَسُبُّوا اللّٰهَ عَدْوًاۢ بِغَيْرِ عِلْمٍ ؕ
كَذٰلِكَ زَيَّنَّا لِكُلِّ اُمَّةٍ عَمَلَهُمْ ۪ ثُمَّ
اِلٰى رَبِّهِمْ مَّرْجِعُهُمْ فَيُنَبِّئُهُمْ بِمَا
كَانُوْا يَعْمَلُوْنَ ﴿١٠٨﴾

Your Guardian–Lord is Allah,
Who created the heavens and
the earth in six stages, and is
firmly established on the throne
(of authority): He draws the night as
a veil over the day, each seeking the
other in rapid succession: He created
the Sun, the Moon, and the stars, (all)
governed by laws under His command.
Is it not His to create and to govern?
Blessed be Allah, the Cherisher and
Sustainer of the worlds!

7:54

اِنَّ رَبَّكُمُ اللّٰهُ الَّذِىْ خَلَقَ
السَّمٰوٰتِ وَالْاَرْضَ فِىْ سِتَّةِ اَيَّامٍ
ثُمَّ اسْتَوٰى عَلَى الْعَرْشِ قف يُغْشِى
الَّيْلَ النَّهَارَ يَطْلُبُهٗ حَثِيْثًا لا وَّ
الشَّمْسَ وَالْقَمَرَ وَالنُّجُوْمَ مُسَخَّرٰتٍۭ
بِاَمْرِهٖ ط اَلَا لَهُ الْخَلْقُ وَالْاَمْرُ ط
تَبٰرَكَ اللّٰهُ رَبُّ الْعٰلَمِيْنَ ﴿٥٤﴾

Say (O Messenger): "O mankind! I am sent to you all, as the Messenger of Allah, to Whom belongs the dominion of the heavens and the earth: there is no authority but He: it is He That gives both life and death. So believe in Allah and His Messenger, the Unlettered Prophet, who believes in Allah and His Revelation (Quran): follow him so that you may be guided."

7:158

قُلْ يَآيُّهَا النَّاسُ اِنِّیْ رَسُوْلُ
اللّٰهِ اِلَيْكُمْ جَمِيْعًا الَّذِیْ لَهٗ مُلْكُ
السَّمٰوٰتِ وَالْاَرْضِ ۚ لَآ اِلٰهَ اِلَّا
هُوَ يُحْيٖ وَيُمِيْتُ ۖ فَاٰمِنُوْا بِاللّٰهِ
وَرَسُوْلِهِ النَّبِیِّ الْاُمِّیِّ الَّذِیْ يُؤْمِنُ
بِاللّٰهِ وَكَلِمٰتِهٖ وَاتَّبِعُوْهُ لَعَلَّكُمْ
تَهْتَدُوْنَ ﴿١٥٨﴾

Say to them (O Muhammad): "Those on whom you call besides Allah are human beings like your own selves. If you believe that they have any supernatural powers, call on them and see if they answer your call and fulfil your desire."

7:194

إِنَّ الَّذِيْنَ تَدْعُوْنَ مِنْ دُوْنِ اللّٰهِ عِبَادٌ
اَمْثَالُكُمْ فَادْعُوْهُمْ فَلْيَسْتَجِيْبُوْا
لَكُمْ إِنْ كُنْتُمْ صٰدِقِيْنَ ﴿١٩٤﴾

Those who are with your Sustainer (Rabb), are never too proud to serve Him. They strive to establish His glory on earth by adoring Him and submitting to His command.

7:206

اِنَّ الَّذِيْنَ عِنْدَ رَبِّكَ لَا يَسْتَكْبِرُوْنَ
عَنْ عِبَادَتِهٖ وَ يُسَبِّحُوْنَهٗ وَلَهٗ
يَسْجُدُوْنَ ع السجدة ٢٠٦

Would you, perchance, fail to fight against people who have broken their solemn pledges, and have done all that they could to drive the Messenger away, and have been first to attack you? Do you fear them ? Nay, it is Allah alone of whom you ought to stand in fear, if you are truly believers!

9:13

اَلَا تُقٰتِلُوْنَ قَوْمًا نَّكَثُوْٓا اَيْمَانَهُمْ
وَهَمُّوْا بِاِخْرَاجِ الرَّسُوْلِ وَهُمْ
بَدَءُوْكُمْ اَوَّلَ مَرَّةٍ ط اَتَخْشَوْنَهُمْ ج
فَاللّٰهُ اَحَقُّ اَنْ تَخْشَوْهُ اِنْ كُنْتُمْ
مُّؤْمِنِيْنَ ﴿١٣﴾

They have taken their rabbis and
their monks-as well as Christ,
son of Mary–for their lords beside
Allah, although they had been
bidden to worship none but the One
God (Allah) save whom there is no
authority in the universe: the One who
is utterly remote, in His limitless glory,
from anything to which they may
ascribe a share in His divinity!

9:31

اِتَّخَذُوْٓا اَحْبَارَهُمْ وَرُهْبٰنَهُمْ
اَرْبَابًا مِّنْ دُوْنِ اللّٰهِ وَالْمَسِيْحَ ابْنَ
مَرْيَمَ ۚ وَمَآ اُمِرُوْٓا اِلَّا لِيَعْبُدُوْٓا
اِلٰـهًا وَّاحِدًا ۚ لَآ اِلٰهَ اِلَّا هُوَ ۗ
سُبْحٰنَهٗ عَمَّا يُشْرِكُوْنَ ﴿٣١﴾

And do not argue with the
followers of earlier revelation
otherwise than in a most kindly
manner–unless it be such of them
as are bent on evildoing and say:
"We believe in that which has been
bestowed from on high upon us, as
well as that which has been bestowed
upon you: or our God and your God is
one and the same, and it is unto Him
that We (all) surrender ourselves."

9:46

وَلَوْ اَرَادُوا الْخُرُوْجَ لَاَعَدُّوْا لَهٗ عُدَّةً
وَّلٰكِنْ كَرِهَ اللّٰهُ انْبِعَاثَهُمْ فَثَبَّطَهُمْ
وَقِيْلَ اقْعُدُوْا مَعَ الْقٰعِدِيْنَ ﴿٤٦﴾

But, if despite all this, they still turn away, O Messenger say to them, "Allah suffices me. There is no authority but Him. In Him alone I place my trust because He is the Nourisher (Rabb) and commands supremacy over all the things in the universe."

9:129

فَاِنْ تَوَلَّوْا فَقُلْ حَسْبِيَ اللّٰهُ ﻗﺯ لَآ اِلٰهَ
اِلَّا هُوَ ؕ عَلَيْهِ تَوَكَّلْتُ وَهُوَ رَبُّ
الْعَرْشِ الْعَظِيْمِ ﴿١٢٩﴾ ع

Surely your Sustainer (Rabb) is Allah, who created the heavens and the earth in six stages, and is firmly established on the throne (of authority), regulating and governing all things. No intercessor (can plead with Him) except after His leave . This is Allah your Sustainer; therefore serve Him: will you not keep this in mind ?

10:3

اِنَّ رَبَّكُمُ اللّٰهُ الَّذِیْ خَلَقَ
السَّمٰوٰتِ وَالْاَرْضَ فِیْ سِتَّةِ
اَیَّامٍ ثُمَّ اسْتَوٰی عَلَی الْعَرْشِ یُدَبِّرُ
الْاَمْرَ ؕ مَا مِنْ شَفِیْعٍ اِلَّا مِنْۢ بَعْدِ
اِذْنِهٖ ؕ ذٰلِكُمُ اللّٰهُ رَبُّكُمْ فَاعْبُدُوْهُ ؕ
اَفَلَا تَذَكَّرُوْنَ ﴿۳﴾

He it is Who has made the Sun a (source of) radiant light and the Moon a light (reflected), and has determined for its phases so that you might know how to compute the years and to measure (time). None of this has Allah created without (an inner) truth. Clearly does explain His laws clearly to people of understanding.

10:5

هُوَ الَّذِیۡ جَعَلَ الشَّمۡسَ ضِیَآءً
وَّ الۡقَمَرَ نُوۡرًا وَّ قَدَّرَہٗ مَنَازِلَ
لِتَعۡلَمُوۡا عَدَدَ السِّنِیۡنَ وَ الۡحِسَابَ ؕ
مَا خَلَقَ اللّٰہُ ذٰلِکَ اِلَّا بِالۡحَقِّ ۚ یُفَصِّلُ
الۡاٰیٰتِ لِقَوۡمٍ یَّعۡلَمُوۡنَ ﴿۵﴾

There and then will every human being clearly apprehend what he has done in the past; and all will be brought back to Allah, their true Lord Supreme, and all their false imagery will have forsaken them.

10:30

هُنَالِكَ تَبْلُوْا كُلُّ نَفْسٍ مَّآ
اَسْلَفَتْ وَرُدُّوْٓا اِلَى اللّٰهِ مَوْلٰىهُمُ
الْحَقِّ وَضَلَّ عَنْهُمْ مَّا كَانُوْا
يَفْتَرُوْنَ ﴿٣٠﴾ ع

O Rasool! ask them: "Who nourishes you out of the bounties of the heaven and the earth? Who has bestowed upon you the faculties of hearing and sight? Who in short, regulates the affairs of existence? They will promptly say: "Allah." Then say: "when you acknowledge that Allah's laws control the physical world and life, why do you not adhere to His laws in the social life of humanity?"

10:31

قُلْ مَنْ يَّرْزُقُكُمْ مِّنَ السَّمَآءِ
وَالْاَرْضِ اَمَّنْ يَّمْلِكُ السَّمْعَ
وَ الْاَبْصَارَ وَ مَنْ يُّخْرِجُ الْحَيَّ مِنَ
الْمَيِّتِ وَ يُخْرِجُ الْمَيِّتَ مِنَ الْحَيِّ
وَمَنْ يُّدَبِّرُ الْاَمْرَ ؕ فَسَيَقُوْلُوْنَ
اللّٰهُ ۚ فَقُلْ اَفَلَا تَتَّقُوْنَ ﴿٣١﴾

Such, then is your Allah (whose laws control the physical world and the life of human beings). These laws are based on truth. Reflect on what the result of discarding Allah's laws would be except to follow the wrong path. So you judge for yourself which way you are following.

10:32

فَذٰلِكُمُ اللّٰهُ رَبُّكُمُ الْحَقُّ ج فَمَاذَا بَعْدَ
الْحَقِّ اِلَّا الضَّلٰلُ ۚ فَاَنّٰى تُصْرَفُوْنَ ﴿٣٢﴾

Say (Muhammad): “O mankind! If you are in doubt as to what my faith is, then (know that) I do not obey those authorities whom you obey beside Allah, but (that) I obey Allah alone, who controls life and death and I am commanded by Him to be among those who believe (in Him alone).”

10:104

قُلْ يٰٓاَيُّهَا النَّاسُ اِنْ كُنْتُمْ فِيْ شَكٍّ
مِّنْ دِيْنِيْ فَلَآ اَعْبُدُ الَّذِيْنَ تَعْبُدُوْنَ
مِنْ دُوْنِ اللّٰهِ وَلٰكِنْ اَعْبُدُ اللّٰهَ الَّذِيْ
يَتَوَفّٰىكُمْ ۖۚ وَاُمِرْتُ اَنْ اَكُوْنَ مِنَ
الْمُؤْمِنِيْنَ ﴿١٠٤﴾ لا

And (know that) if Allah should
touch you with misfortune, there
is none who could remove it except
Him; and if He intends good for you,
there is none who could turn away His
bounty: He causes it to alight upon
whomsoever He wills of His servants.
And He alone is truly forgiving, truly
a dispenser of grace.

10:107

وَإِنْ يَّمْسَسْكَ اللّٰهُ بِضُرٍّ
فَلَا كَاشِفَ لَهٗٓ إِلَّا هُوَ ۚ وَإِنْ يُّرِدْكَ
بِخَيْرٍ فَلَا رَآدَّ لِفَضْلِهٖ ؕ يُصِيْبُ بِهٖ
مَنْ يَّشَآءُ مِنْ عِبَادِهٖ ؕ وَهُوَ الْغَفُوْرُ
الرَّحِيْمُ ﴿١٠٧﴾

And if they (the false gods whom you have called to your aid) are not able to help you, then know that (this Quran) has been bestowed from on high out of Allah's wisdom alone, and that there is no deity save Him. Will you, then, surrender yourselves unto Him?"

11:14

فَاِلَّمْ يَسْتَجِيْبُوْا لَكُمْ فَاعْلَمُوْٓا

اَنَّمَآ اُنْزِلَ بِعِلْمِ اللّٰهِ وَاَنْ لَّآ اِلٰهَ اِلَّا

هُوَ ۚ فَهَلْ اَنْتُمْ مُّسْلِمُوْنَ ﴿١٤﴾

And Allah alone comprehends the hidden reality of the heavens and the earth: for, all that exists goes back to Him (as its source). Obey and worship Him, then, and place your trust in Him alone: for your Sustainer (Rabb) is aware of what you do.

11:123

وَ لِلّٰهِ غَيْبُ السَّمٰوٰتِ وَ الْاَرْضِ
وَ اِلَيْهِ يُرْجَعُ الْاَمْرُ كُلُّهٗ فَاعْبُدْهُ
وَتَوَكَّلْ عَلَيْهِ ؕ وَمَا رَبُّكَ بِغٰفِلٍ
عَمَّا تَعْمَلُوْنَ ﴿۱۲۳﴾ ع

(O Messenger) We have sent you as We sent the Messengers before you so that you convey to them what We reveal to you, for in their ignorance, they deny the Most Gracious. Say, “He is my Sustainer, there is no god but He. In Him I put my trust and to Him do I turn (for grace)

13:30

كَذٰلِكَ اَرْسَلْنٰكَ فِيْٓ اُمَّةٍ قَدْ خَلَتْ
مِنْ قَبْلِهَآ اُمَمٌ لِّتَتْلُوَاْ عَلَيْهِمُ
الَّذِيْٓ اَوْحَيْنَآ اِلَيْكَ وَهُمْ يَكْفُرُوْنَ
بِالرَّحْمٰنِ ؕ قُلْ هُوَ رَبِّيْ لَآ اِلٰهَ اِلَّا هُوَ ۚ
عَلَيْهِ تَوَكَّلْتُ وَاِلَيْهِ مَتَابِ ﴿٣٠﴾

Those to whom We have given the Book (Quran) rejoice at what has been revealed to you: but there are among the clans those who reject a part thereof. Say: "I am commanded to worship Allah, and not to join partners with Him. Unto Him do I call, and to Him is my return."

13:36

وَالَّذِيْنَ اٰتَيْنٰهُمُ الْكِتٰبَ يَفْرَحُوْنَ
بِمَآ اُنْزِلَ اِلَيْكَ وَمِنَ الْاَحْزَابِ مَنْ
يُّنْكِرُ بَعْضَهٗ ؕ قُلْ اِنَّمَآ اُمِرْتُ اَنْ
اَعْبُدَ اللّٰهَ وَلَآ اُشْرِكَ بِهٖ ؕ اِلَيْهِ اَدْعُوْا
وَاِلَيْهِ مَاٰبِ ﴿٣٦﴾

Do you not see that Allah created the heavens and the earth in Truth? If He so will, He can remove you and put in your place a new creation?

14:19

اَلَمْ تَرَ اَنَّ اللّٰهَ خَلَقَ السَّمٰوٰتِ وَ
الْاَرْضَ بِالْحَقِّ ؕ اِنْ يَّشَاْ يُذْهِبْكُمْ
وَيَاْتِ بِخَلْقٍ جَدِيْدٍ ۙ﴿١٩﴾

Here is a Message for mankind: Let them take warning from it, and let them know that He is (no other than) One Allah, let men of understanding take heed.

14:52

هٰذَا بَلٰغٌ لِّلنَّاسِ وَلِيُنْذَرُوْا بِهٖ
وَلِيَعْلَمُوْٓا اَنَّمَا هُوَ اِلٰهٌ وَّاحِدٌ
وَّلِيَذَّكَّرَ اُولُوا الْاَلْبٰبِ ۝ ع ٥٢

Tell My servants that I–I alone–
am truly forgiving, a true dispenser
of Grace.

15:49

نَبِّئْ عِبَادِيٓ اَنِّيٓ اَنَا الْغَفُوْرُ الرَّحِيْمُ ﴿۴۹﴾ لا

And remember: We have not
created the heavens and the earth
and all that is between them without
purpose but, behold, the Hour
(when this will become clear to all)
is indeed yet to come. Hence, forgive
(O Muhammad) men's failings and
forgive them graciously.

15:85

وَمَا خَلَقْنَا السَّمٰوٰتِ وَالْاَرْضَ
وَمَا بَيْنَهُمَآ اِلَّا بِالْحَقِّ ؕ وَاِنَّ
السَّاعَةَ لَاٰتِيَةٌ فَاصْفَحِ الصَّفْحَ
الْجَمِيْلَ ﴿۸۵﴾

But celebrate the praises of thy Lord, and be of those who prostrate themselves in adoration. Obey and worship your Sustainer (Rabb) till death comes to you.

15:98, 99

فَسَبِّحْ بِحَمْدِ رَبِّكَ وَكُنْ مِّنَ
السّٰجِدِيْنَ ﴿٩٨﴾ وَاعْبُدْ رَبَّكَ حَتّٰى
يَاْتِيَكَ الْيَقِيْنُ ﴿٩٩﴾

Truly, Allah knows all that they keep secret as well as all that they bring into the open–(and,) behold, He does not love those who are given to arrogance; When it is said to them, "What is it that your Sustainer (Rabb) has revealed?" they say, "Tales of the ancients!"

16:23, 24

لَا جَرَمَ اَنَّ اللّٰهَ يَعْلَمُ مَا يُسِرُّوْنَ
وَمَا يُعْلِنُوْنَ ؕ اِنَّهٗ لَا يُحِبُّ
الْمُسْتَكْبِرِيْنَ ﴿۲۳﴾ وَاِذَا قِيْلَ لَهُمْ
مَّاذَآ اَنْزَلَ رَبُّكُمْ ۙ قَالُوْٓا اَسَاطِيْرُ
الْاَوَّلِيْنَ ۙ﴿۲۴﴾

So eat of the lawful and good food
which Allah has provided for you,
and render thanks unto Allah for
His blessings, if it is (truly) Him that
you worship.

16:114

فَكُلُوْا مِمَّا رَزَقَكُمُ اللّٰهُ حَلٰلًا
طَيِّبًا ۖ وَّ اشْكُرُوْا نِعْمَتَ اللّٰهِ اِنْ
كُنْتُمْ اِيَّاهُ تَعْبُدُوْنَ ﴿١١٤﴾

And to those who believe not in the Hereafter, (it announceth) that We have prepared for them a Penalty Grievous (indeed).

17:10

وَّاَنَّ الَّذِیۡنَ لَا یُؤۡمِنُوۡنَ بِالۡاٰخِرَۃِ
اَعۡتَدۡنَا لَهُمۡ عَذَابًا اَلِیۡمًا ﴿۱۰﴾ ع

How many generations have We destroyed after Noah? and enough is thy Sustainer to note and see the sins of His servants.

17:17

وَكَمْ اَهْلَكْنَا مِنَ الْقُرُوْنِ مِنْۢ بَعْدِ
نُوْحٍ ؕ وَكَفٰى بِرَبِّكَ بِذُنُوْبِ عِبَادِهٖ
خَبِيْرًۢا بَصِيْرًا ﴿١٧﴾

Do not set up any other god side by side with Allah, if you do you will yourself be disgraced and forsaken.

17:22

لَا تَجْعَلْ مَعَ اللّٰهِ اِلٰـهًا اٰخَرَ فَتَقْعُدَ
مَذْمُوْمًا مَّخْذُوْلًا ﴿٢٢﴾ ع

Your Sustainer (Rabb) has ordained that you shall worship none but Him. And do good to your parents. Should one of them, or both, attain to old age in thy care, never say "Ugh" to them or scold them, but (always) speak unto them with reverent and gracious speech; and spread over them humbly the wings of your tenderness, and say: "O my Sustainer! Bestow Your Grace upon them, even as they cherished and reared me when I was a child!"

17:23, 24

وَقَضٰى رَبُّكَ اَلَّا تَعۡبُدُوۡۤا اِلَّاۤ
اِيَّاهُ وَبِالۡوٰلِدَيۡنِ اِحۡسٰنًا ؕ اِمَّا
يَبۡلُغَنَّ عِنۡدَكَ الۡكِبَرَ اَحَدُهُمَاۤ
اَوۡ كِلٰهُمَا فَلَا تَقُلۡ لَّهُمَاۤ اُفٍّ وَّلَا
تَنۡهَرۡهُمَا وَقُلۡ لَّهُمَا قَوۡلًا كَرِيۡمًا ﴿٢٣﴾ وَ
اخۡفِضۡ لَهُمَا جَنَاحَ الذُّلِّ مِنَ الرَّحۡمَةِ
وَقُلۡ رَّبِّ ارۡحَمۡهُمَا كَمَا رَبَّيٰنِيۡ
صَغِيۡرًا ؕ ﴿٢٤﴾

Behold, your Sustainer (Rabb) grants abundant sustenance, or gives it in scant measure, to whomever He wills: surely He is fully aware of (the needs of) His creatures, and sees them all.

17:30

اِنَّ رَبَّكَ يَبْسُطُ الرِّزْقَ لِمَنْ يَّشَآءُ
وَ يَقْدِرُ ؕ اِنَّهٗ كَانَ بِعِبَادِهٖ خَبِيْرًۢا
بَصِيْرًا ﴿۳۰﴾ ع

This is part of that knowledge of right and wrong with which thy Sustainer has inspired thee. Hence, do not set up any other authority or god side by side with Allah, if you do so be forewarned that you will be cast into hell, blameworthy and rejected by Him.

17:39

ذٰلِكَ مِمَّآ اَوۡحٰۤى اِلَيۡكَ رَبُّكَ مِنَ
الۡحِكۡمَةِ ؕ وَلَا تَجۡعَلۡ مَعَ اللّٰهِ
اِلٰـهًا اٰخَرَ فَتُلۡقٰى فِىۡ جَهَنَّمَ مَلُوۡمًا
مَّدۡحُوۡرًا ﴿۳۹﴾

These people say that Allah has associates whom they have set up as peers to Him. O Rasool! tell them that had this been the case, these so-called associates would have devised means to share with Allah the control of the universe. In that event there would have been utter chaos.

17:42

قُلْ لَّوْ كَانَ مَعَهٗۤ اٰلِـهَةٌ كَمَا يَقُوْلُوْنَ اِذًا
لَّابْتَغَوْا اِلٰى ذِى الْعَرْشِ سَبِيْلًا ﴿٤٢﴾

Say (O Muhammad): "Call upon Allah, or call upon Rahman: by whatever name ye call upon Him, (it is well): for to Him belong the Most Beautiful Names. Neither speak your Prayer aloud, nor speak it in a low tone, but seek a middle course between."

17:110

قُلِ ادْعُوا اللّٰهَ اَوِ ادْعُوا الرَّحْمٰنَ
اَيًّا مَّا تَدْعُوْا فَلَهُ الْاَسْمَآءُ ط
الْحُسْنٰى ج وَلَا تَجْهَرْ بِصَلَاتِكَ
وَلَا تُخَافِتْ بِهَا وَابْتَغِ بَيْنَ ذٰلِكَ
سَبِيْلًا ﴿١١٠﴾

We gave strength to their hearts:
Behold, they stood up and said: “Our Sustainer (Rabb) is the Sustainer of the heavens and of the earth: never shall we call upon any god other than Him: if we did, we should indeed have uttered a big blunder”.

18:14

وَّرَبَطْنَا عَلٰى قُلُوْبِهِمْ اِذْ قَامُوْا
فَقَالُوْا رَبُّنَا رَبُّ السَّمٰوٰتِ وَ
الْاَرْضِ لَنْ نَّدْعُوَاْ مِنْ دُوْنِهٖٓ اِلٰـهًا لَّقَدْ
قُلْنَآ اِذًا شَطَطًا ﴿۱۴﴾

Do they who are bent on denying the truth think, perchance, that they could take (any of) My creatures for protectors against Me? Surely, We have readied hell to welcome all who deny the truth!

18:102

اَفَحَسِبَ الَّذِيْنَ كَفَرُوْٓا اَنْ يَّتَّخِذُوْا
عِبَادِيْ مِنْ دُوْنِيْٓ اَوْلِيَآءَ ؕ اِنَّـآ اَعْتَدْنَا
جَهَنَّمَ لِلْكٰفِرِيْنَ نُزُلًا ﴿۱۰۲﴾

Say: (O Messenger) “I am only
a mortal like you. My Sustainer
(Rabb) inspireth in me that your
Allah is only One Allah. And whoever
hopeth for the meeting with his
Sustainer, let him do righteous work,
and make none sharer of the worship
due unto his Sustainer (Rabb).”

18:110

قُلْ اِنَّمَآ اَنَا بَشَرٌ مِّثْلُكُمْ يُوْحٰٓى
اِلَيَّ اَنَّمَآ اِلٰـهُكُمْ اِلٰهٌ وَّاحِدٌ ۚ فَمَنْ
كَانَ يَرْجُوْا لِقَآءَ رَبِّهٖ فَلْيَعْمَلْ
عَمَلًا صَالِحًا وَّلَا يُشْرِكْ بِعِبَادَةِ رَبِّهٖٓ
اَحَدًا ﴿١١٠﴾ ع

The Sustainer (Rabb) of the heavens and the earth and all that is between them! Worship, then, Him alone, and remain steadfast in His worship! Do you know any whose name is worthy to be mentioned side by side with His?"

19:65

رَبُّ السَّمٰوٰتِ وَالْاَرْضِ وَمَا
بَيْنَهُمَا فَاعْبُدْهُ وَاصْطَبِرْ لِعِبٰدَتِهٖ ؕ
هَلْ تَعْلَمُ لَهٗ سَمِيًّا ﴿۶۵﴾ ع

Allah. there is no authority but He!
To Him belong the most Beautiful
Names (His alone are the Attributes
of perfection).

20:8

اَللّٰہُ لَآ اِلٰہَ اِلَّا ھُوَ ؕ لَہُ الۡاَسۡمَآءُ
الۡحُسۡنٰی ﴿۸﴾

Your God is only Allah. There is no other God He embraces all things in His knowledge.

20:98

اِنَّمَآ اِلٰـهُـكُمُ اللّٰهُ الَّذِیْ لَآ اِلٰهَ اِلَّا هُوَ ؕ

وَسِعَ كُلَّ شَیْءٍ عِلْمًا ﴿۹۸﴾

(Know,) then, (that) Allah is sublimely exalted, the Ultimate Sovereign, the Ultimate Truth and (knowing this,) do not approach the Quran in haste, before it has been revealed to you in full, but (always) say: "O my Sustainer (Rabb), increase me in my knowledge!"

20:114

فَتَعٰلَى اللّٰهُ الْمَلِكُ الْحَقُّ ۚ وَلَا تَعْجَلْ
بِالْقُرْاٰنِ مِنْ قَبْلِ اَنْ يُّقْضٰٓى اِلَيْكَ
وَحْيُهٗ ۡ وَقُلْ رَّبِّ زِدْنِيْ عِلْمًا ﴿١١٤﴾

And (know that) We have not created the heavens and the earth and all that is between them in mere idle play:

21:16

وَمَا خَلَقْنَا السَّمَآءَ وَالْأَرْضَ وَمَا
بَيْنَهُمَا لَٰعِبِينَ ﴿١٦﴾

Had there been in heaven or on earth any deities Supreme Authority other than Allah, both (those realms would surely have fallen into ruin! But limitless in His glory is Allah, enthroned in His awesome almightiness far above anything that men may devise by way of definition!

21:22

لَوۡ كَانَ فِيۡهِمَاۤ اٰلِهَةٌ اِلَّا اللّٰهُ لَفَسَدَتَا ۚ
فَسُبۡحٰنَ اللّٰهِ رَبِّ الۡعَرۡشِ عَمَّا
يَصِفُوۡنَ ﴿۲۲﴾

Say: “What has come to me by inspiration is that your Allah is One Allah. will you therefore bow to His Will (in Islam)?”

21:108

قُلْ اِنَّمَا يُوْحٰٓى اِلَيَّ اَنَّمَآ اِلٰهُكُمْ اِلٰهٌ
وّٰحِدٌ ۚ فَهَلْ اَنْتُمْ مُّسْلِمُوْنَ ﴿١٠٨﴾

O mankind!
if ye have a doubt
about the Resurrection,
(consider) that We created you
out of dust, then out of sperm,
then out of a leech-like clot, then
out of a morsel of flesh, partly formed
and partly unformed, in order that We
may manifest (our power) to you; and We
cause whom We will to rest in the wombs
for an appointed term, then do We bring
you out as babes, then (foster you) that ye
may reach your age of full strength; and
some of you are called to die, and some are
sent back to the feeblest old age, so that
they know nothing after having known
(much), and (further), thou seest the
earth barren and lifeless, but when We
pour down rain on it, it is stirred (to
life), it swells, and it puts forth
every kind of beautiful growth
(in pairs).

22:5

يَآ اَيُّهَا النَّاسُ اِنْ كُنْتُمْ

فِيْ رَيْبٍ مِّنَ الْبَعْثِ فَاِنَّا

خَلَقْنٰكُمْ مِّنْ تُرَابٍ ثُمَّ مِنْ نُّطْفَةٍ ثُمَّ

مِنْ عَلَقَةٍ ثُمَّ مِنْ مُّضْغَةٍ مُّخَلَّقَةٍ وَّ غَيْرِ مُخَلَّقَةٍ

لِّنُبَيِّنَ لَكُمْ ؕ وَ نُقِرُّ فِى الْاَرْحَامِ مَا نَشَآءُ اِلٰٓى اَجَلٍ

مُّسَمًّى ثُمَّ نُخْرِجُكُمْ طِفْلًا ثُمَّ لِتَبْلُغُوْٓا اَشُدَّكُمْ ۚ

وَ مِنْكُمْ مَّنْ يُّتَوَفّٰى وَ مِنْكُمْ مَّنْ يُّرَدُّ اِلٰٓى اَرْذَلِ

الْعُمُرِ لِكَيْلَا يَعْلَمَ مِنْۢ بَعْدِ عِلْمٍ شَيْئًا ؕ وَ تَرَى

الْاَرْضَ هَامِدَةً فَاِذَآ اَنْزَلْنَا عَلَيْهَا الْمَآءَ

اهْتَزَّتْ وَ رَبَتْ وَ اَنْۢبَتَتْ مِنْ كُلِّ

زَوْجٍۢ بَهِيْجٍ ﴿٥﴾

This is so, because Allah is the Reality:
it is He Who gives life to the dead,
and it is He Who has power over
all things.

22:6

ذٰلِكَ بِاَنَّ اللّٰهَ هُوَ الۡحَقُّ وَ اَنَّهٗ يُحۡيِ
الۡمَوۡتٰى وَ اَنَّهٗ عَلٰى كُلِّ شَىۡءٍ قَدِيۡرٌ ۙ﴿۶﴾

(It will be said): "This is because of the deeds which thy hands sent forth, for verily Allah is not unjust to His servants."

22:10

ذٰلِكَ بِمَا قَدَّمَتْ يَدَاكَ وَ اَنَّ اللّٰهَ لَيْسَ
بِظَلَّامٍ لِّلْعَبِيْدِ ﴿١٠﴾ ع

And among people there are those who serve Allah conditionally. If things go their way, they are satisfied. But if some adversity touches them they turn their faces away, losing both, this world and the hereafter. Indeed it is a loss beyond compare.

22:11

وَ مِنَ النَّاسِ مَنْ يَّعْبُدُ اللّٰهَ عَلٰى
حَرْفٍ ۚ فَاِنْ اَصَابَهٗ خَيْرُ نِ اطْمَاَنَّ
بِهٖ ۚ وَاِنْ اَصَابَتْهُ فِتْنَةُ نِ انْقَلَبَ عَلٰى
وَجْهِهٖ ۚ قف خَسِرَ الدُّنْيَا وَالْاٰخِرَةَ ؕ
ذٰلِكَ هُوَ الْخُسْرَانُ الْمُبِيْنُ ﴿۱۱﴾

That is because Allah–He is the Reality; and those besides Him whom they invoke,–they are but vain Falsehood: verily Allah is He, Most High, Most Great.

22:62

ذٰلِكَ بِاَنَّ اللّٰهَ هُوَ الْحَقُّ وَ اَنَّ مَا
يَدْعُوْنَ مِنْ دُوْنِهٖ هُوَ الْبٰطِلُ وَ اَنَّ
اللّٰهَ هُوَ الْعَلِيُّ الْكَبِيْرُ ﴿٦٢﴾

Knowest thou not that Allah knows all that is in heaven and on earth? Indeed it is all in a Record, and that is easy for Allah. Yet they worship, besides Allah, things for which no authority has been sent down to them, and of which they have (really) no knowledge: for those that do wrong there is no helper.

22:70, 71

اَلَمْ تَعْلَمْ اَنَّ اللّٰهَ يَعْلَمُ مَا فِي
السَّمَآءِ وَ الْاَرْضِ ؕ اِنَّ ذٰلِكَ فِيْ
كِتٰبٍ ؕ اِنَّ ذٰلِكَ عَلَى اللّٰهِ يَسِيْرٌ ﴿٧٠﴾ وَ
يَعْبُدُوْنَ مِنْ دُوْنِ اللّٰهِ مَا لَمْ يُنَزِّلْ بِهٖ
سُلْطٰنًا وَّ مَا لَيْسَ لَهُمْ بِهٖ عِلْمٌ ؕ وَمَا
لِلظّٰلِمِيْنَ مِنْ نَّصِيْرٍ ﴿٧١﴾

O you who have attained to faith!
Bow down and prostrate yourselves,
and worship your Sustainer (alone),
and do good, so that you might attain
to a happy state!

22:77

يٰاَيُّهَا الَّذِيْنَ اٰمَنُوا ارْكَعُوْا
وَاسْجُدُوْا وَاعْبُدُوْا رَبَّكُمْ
وَافْعَلُوا الْخَيْرَ لَعَلَّكُمْ تُفْلِحُوْنَ ج السجدة ٧٧

Never did Allah take unto Himself any offspring, nor has there ever been any deity side by side with Him: (for, had there been any,) lo! each deity would surely have stood apart (from the others) in whatever it had created, and they would surely have (tried to) overcome one another! Limitless in His glory is Allah, (far) above anything that men may devise by way of definition,He over all that they ascribe as partners (unto Him)!

23:91

مَا اتَّخَذَ اللّٰهُ مِنْ وَّلَدٍ وَّمَا كَانَ مَعَهٗ
مِنْ اِلٰهٍ اِذًا لَّذَهَبَ كُلُّ اِلٰهٍۭ بِمَا خَلَقَ
وَ لَعَلَا بَعْضُهُمْ عَلٰى بَعْضٍ ؕ سُبْحٰنَ
اللّٰهِ عَمَّا يَصِفُوْنَ ۙ﴿٩١﴾

(Know) then, (that) Allah is sublimely exalted, the Ultimate Sovereign, the Ultimate Truth: there is no deity save Him, the Sustainer, in bountiful almightiness enthroned!

23:116

فَتَعٰلَى اللّٰهُ الْمَلِكُ الْحَقُّ ۚ لَآ اِلٰهَ اِلَّا
هُوَ ۚ رَبُّ الْعَرْشِ الْكَرِيْمِ ﴿١١٦﴾

On that day (of resurrection) Allah will pay them in full their just due, and they will come to know that Allah alone is the Ultimate Truth, manifest, and manifesting (the true nature of all that has ever been done)

24:25

يَوۡمَئِذٍ يُّوَفِّيۡهِمُ اللّٰهُ دِيۡنَهُمُ الۡحَقَّ وَ
يَعۡلَمُوۡنَ اَنَّ اللّٰهَ هُوَ الۡحَقُّ الۡمُبِيۡنُ ﴿۲۵﴾

Allah has promised,
to those among you who
believe and work righteous
deeds, that He will, of a surety,
grant them in the land, inheritance
(of power), as He granted it to those
before them; that He will establish in
authority their religion–the one which
He has chosen for them; and that
He will change (their state), after the
fear in which they (lived), to one of
security and peace: They will worship
Me (alone) and not associate aught
with Me. If any do reject Faith
after this, they are rebellious
and wicked.

24:55

وَعَدَ اللّٰهُ الَّذِيْنَ
اٰمَنُوْا مِنْكُمْ وَعَمِلُوا
الصّٰلِحٰتِ لَيَسْتَخْلِفَنَّهُمْ فِي
الْاَرْضِ كَمَا اسْتَخْلَفَ الَّذِيْنَ
مِنْ قَبْلِهِمْ ۖ وَلَيُمَكِّنَنَّ لَهُمْ دِيْنَهُمُ
الَّذِى ارْتَضٰى لَهُمْ وَلَيُبَدِّلَنَّهُمْ مِّنْۢ
بَعْدِ خَوْفِهِمْ اَمْنًا ۭ يَعْبُدُوْنَنِيْ
لَا يُشْرِكُوْنَ بِيْ شَيْـًٔا ۭ وَمَنْ
كَفَرَ بَعْدَ ذٰلِكَ فَاُولٰٓئِكَ هُمُ
الْفٰسِقُوْنَ ﴿٥٥﴾

And put thy trust in Him Who lives and dies not; and celebrate his praise; and enough is He to be acquainted with the faults of His servants;

25:58

وَ تَوَكَّلْ عَلَى الْحَيِّ الَّذِيْ لَا يَمُوْتُ

وَ سَبِّحْ بِحَمْدِهٖ ؕ وَكَفٰى بِهٖ بِذُنُوْبِ

عِبَادِهٖ خَبِيْرًا ۚۙ ﴿۵۸﴾

He Who created the heavens and the earth and all that is between, in six days, and is firmly established on the Throne (of Authority): Allah Most Gracious: ask , then, about Him, (the) One who is (truly) aware.

25:59

الَّذِیْ خَلَقَ السَّمٰوٰتِ وَ الْاَرْضَ وَ
مَا بَیْنَهُمَا فِیْ سِتَّةِ اَیَّامٍ ثُمَّ اسْتَوٰی
عَلَی الْعَرْشِ ۛۚ اَلرَّحْمٰنُ فَسْـَٔلْ بِهٖ
خَبِیْرًا ﴿۵۹﴾

But (as for thee, O believer,) surely, you have received this Quran out of the Grace of One who is wise, all-knowing.

27:6

وَ اِنَّكَ لَتُلَقَّى الْقُرْاٰنَ مِنْ لَّدُنْ
حَكِيْمٍ عَلِيْمٍ ۝٦

"There is no supreme authority but Allah!–and He is Sustainer of the Throne Supreme!"

27:26

اَللّٰهُ لَآ اِلٰهَ اِلَّا هُوَ رَبُّ الْعَرْشِ
الْعَظِيْمِ ﴿٢٦﴾ السجدة

Say: “Praise be to Allah, and Peace on his servants whom He has chosen (for his Message). (Who) is better?– Allah or the false gods they associate (with Him)?

27:59

قُلِ الْحَمْدُ لِلّٰهِ وَسَلٰمٌ عَلٰى عِبَادِهِ
الَّذِيْنَ اصْطَفٰى ؕ آٰللّٰهُ خَيْرٌ اَمَّا
يُشْرِكُوْنَ ؕ ﴿۵۹﴾

Who is it that has created
the heavens and the earth, and
sends down for you (life-giving
water from the skies? For it is by
this means that We cause gardens
of shining beauty to grow–(whereas)
it is not in your power to cause (even
one single of) its trees to grow! Could
there be any Divine power besides
Allah? No, they (who think so) are
people who swerve (from the path
of reason)

27:60

اَمَّنْ خَلَقَ السَّمٰوٰتِ وَالْاَرْضَ
وَ اَنْزَلَ لَكُمْ مِّنَ السَّمَآءِ مَآءً ۚ
فَاَنْۢبَتْنَا بِهٖ حَدَآئِقَ ذَاتَ بَهْجَةٍ ۚ مَا
كَانَ لَكُمْ اَنْ تُنْۢبِتُوْا شَجَرَهَا ؕ ءَاِلٰهٌ
مَّعَ اللّٰهِ ؕ بَلْ هُمْ قَوْمٌ يَّعْدِلُوْنَ ؕ ﴿٦٠﴾

Who is it that has made the earth a fitting abode (for living things), and has caused running waters (to flow) in its midst, and has set upon it mountains firm, and has placed a barrier between the two great bodies of water? Could there be any Divine power besides Allah? Nay, most of those (who think so) do not know (what they are saying)!

27:61

اَمَّنْ جَعَلَ الْاَرْضَ قَرَارًا وَّ جَعَلَ
خِلٰلَهَآ اَنْهٰرًا وَّ جَعَلَ لَهَا رَوٰسِیَ وَ
جَعَلَ بَیْنَ الْبَحْرَیْنِ حَاجِزًا ؕ ءَاِلٰهٌ مَّعَ
اللّٰهِ ؕ بَلْ اَكْثَرُهُمْ لَا یَعْلَمُوْنَ ﴿٦١﴾

Who is it that responds to the distressed when he calls out to Him, and Who removes the ill that caused the distress, and has made you inherit the earth? Could there be any Divine power besides Allah? How seldom do you keep this in mind!

27:62

اَمَّنۡ يُّجِيۡبُ الۡمُضۡطَرَّ اِذَا دَعَاهُ وَ
يَكۡشِفُ السُّوۡٓءَ وَ يَجۡعَلُكُمۡ خُلَفَآءَ
الۡاَرۡضِ ؕ ءَاِلٰهٌ مَّعَ اللّٰهِ ؕ قَلِيۡلًا مَّا
تَذَكَّرُوۡنَ ؕ﴿۶۲﴾

Who is it that guides you in the midst of the deep darkness of land and sea, and sends forth the winds as a glad tiding of His coming Grace? Could there be any Divine power besides Allah? Sublimely exalted is God above anything to which men may ascribe a share in His Divinity!

27:63

اَمَّنْ يَّهْدِيْكُمْ فِيْ ظُلُمٰتِ الْبَرِّ وَ
الْبَحْرِ وَ مَنْ يُّرْسِلُ الرِّيٰحَ بُشْرًۢا بَيْنَ
يَدَيْ رَحْمَتِهٖ ؕ ءَاِلٰهٌ مَّعَ اللّٰهِ ؕ تَعٰلَى
اللّٰهُ عَمَّا يُشْرِكُوْنَ ﴿٦٣﴾ؕ

Who is it that creates all life in the first instance, and then brings it forth anew? And who is it that provides you with sustenance out of heaven and earth? Could there be any Divine power besides Allah? Say: "(If you think so,) produce your evidence - if you truly believe in your claim!"

27:64

اَمَّنۡ يَّبۡدَؤُا الۡخَلۡقَ ثُمَّ يُعِيۡدُهٗ وَ مَنۡ
يَّرۡزُقُكُمۡ مِّنَ السَّمَآءِ وَ الۡاَرۡضِ ؕ
ءَاِلٰهٌ مَّعَ اللّٰهِ ؕ قُلۡ هَاتُوۡا بُرۡهَانَكُمۡ اِنۡ
كُنۡتُمۡ صٰدِقِيۡنَ ﴿۶۴﴾

(Say, O Muhammad:) “I have been bidden to worship the Sustainer of this City–Him Who has made it sacred, and to whom all things belong: and I have been bidden to be of those who surrender themselves to Him.

27:91

إِنَّمَآ أُمِرْتُ أَنْ أَعْبُدَ رَبَّ هٰذِهِ الْبَلْدَةِ
الَّذِىْ حَرَّمَهَا وَلَهٗ كُلُّ شَىْءٍ ز وَّأُمِرْتُ
أَنْ أَكُوْنَ مِنَ الْمُسْلِمِيْنَ ﴿٩١﴾ لا

For He is Allah, there is no supreme authority except Him. To Him all praise is due, at the beginning and at the end (of time); and with Him rests all judgment; and to Him you shall all be brought back.

28:70

وَهُوَ اللّٰهُ لَآ اِلٰهَ اِلَّا هُوَ ؕ لَهُ الْحَمْدُ
فِي الْاُوْلٰى وَالْاٰخِرَةِ ۫ وَلَهُ الْحُكْمُ وَ
اِلَيْهِ تُرْجَعُوْنَ ﴿۷۰﴾

Say: “Have you ever considered (this): If Allah had willed that there should always be night about you, without break, until the Day of Resurrection - is there any deity other than Allah that could bring you light? Will you not, then, listen (to the truth)?”

28:71

قُلْ اَرَءَيْتُمْ اِنْ جَعَلَ اللّٰهُ عَلَيْكُمُ
الَّيْلَ سَرْمَدًا اِلٰى يَوْمِ الْقِيٰمَةِ مَنْ
اِلٰهٌ غَيْرُ اللّٰهِ يَاْتِيْكُمْ بِضِيَآءٍ ؕ اَفَلَا
تَسْمَعُوْنَ ﴿٧١﴾

Say: “Have you ever considered (this): If Allah had willed that there should always be daylight about you, without break, until the Day of Resurrection - is there any supreme authority other than Allah that could bring you (the darkness of) night, wherein you might rest? Will you not, then, see (the truth)?

28:72

قُلْ اَرَءَيْتُمْ اِنْ جَعَلَ اللّٰهُ عَلَيْكُمُ
النَّهَارَ سَرْمَدًا اِلٰى يَوْمِ الْقِيٰمَةِ
مَنْ اِلٰهٌ غَيْرُ اللّٰهِ يَاْتِيْكُمْ بِلَيْلٍ
تَسْكُنُوْنَ فِيْهِ ؕ اَفَلَا تُبْصِرُوْنَ ﴿٧٢﴾

Allah created the heavens and the earth in true (proportions): verily in that is a Sign for those who believe.

29:44

خَلَقَ اللّٰهُ السَّمٰوٰتِ وَالْاَرْضَ بِالْحَقِّ ؕ

اِنَّ فِیْ ذٰلِكَ لَاٰیَةً لِّلْمُؤْمِنِیْنَ ﴿٤٤﴾ ع

Say (unto those who will not believe): “Allah is witness enough between me and you! He knows all that is in the heavens and on earth; and they who are bent on believing in what is false and vain, and thus on denying Allah–it is they, they who shall be the losers!”

29:52

قُلْ كَفٰى بِاللّٰهِ بَيْنِىْ وَ بَيْنَكُمْ
شَهِيْدًا ۚ يَعْلَمُ مَا فِى السَّمٰوٰتِ
وَالْاَرْضِ ؕ وَالَّذِيْنَ اٰمَنُوْا بِالْبَاطِلِ
وَكَفَرُوْا بِاللّٰهِ ۙ اُولٰٓئِكَ هُمُ
الْخٰسِرُوْنَ ﴿٥٢﴾

Have they not pondered upon themselves? Allah created not the heavens and the earth, and that which is between them, save with truth and for a destined end them without (an inner) truth and a term set (by Him): and yet, behold, there are many people who stubbornly deny the truth that they are destined to meet their Sustainer (Rabb).

30:8

اَوَلَمْ يَتَفَكَّرُوْا فِيْٓ اَنْفُسِهِمْ قف مَا
خَلَقَ اللّٰهُ السَّمٰوٰتِ وَ الْاَرْضَ وَمَا
بَيْنَهُمَآ اِلَّا بِالْحَقِّ وَ اَجَلٍ مُّسَمًّى ط
وَ اِنَّ كَثِيْرًا مِّنَ النَّاسِ بِلِقَآئِ رَبِّهِمْ
لَكٰفِرُوْنَ ﴿٨﴾

It is Allah Who sends the Winds, and they raise the Clouds: then does He spread them in the sky as He wills, and break them into fragments, until thou sees rain-drops issue from the midst thereof: then when He has made them reach such of his servants as He wills behold, they do rejoice!

30:48

اَللّٰهُ الَّذِیۡ یُرۡسِلُ الرِّیٰحَ فَتُثِیۡرُ سَحَابًا
فَیَبۡسُطُهٗ فِی السَّمَآءِ کَیۡفَ یَشَآءُ وَ
یَجۡعَلُهٗ کِسَفًا فَتَرَی الۡوَدۡقَ یَخۡرُجُ مِنۡ
خِلٰلِهٖ ۚ فَاِذَاۤ اَصَابَ بِهٖ مَنۡ یَّشَآءُ مِنۡ
عِبَادِهٖۤ اِذَا هُمۡ یَسۡتَبۡشِرُوۡنَ ﴿۴۸﴾

Art thou not aware that it is Allah who makes the night grow longer by shortening the day, and makes the day grow longer by shortening the night, and that He has made the sun and the moon subservient (to His laws), each running its course for a term set (by Him) and that Allah is fully aware of all that you do?

31:29

اَلَمْ تَرَ اَنَّ اللّٰهَ يُوْلِجُ الَّيْلَ فِي
النَّهَارِ وَ يُوْلِجُ النَّهَارَ فِي الَّيْلِ
وَ سَخَّرَ الشَّمْسَ وَ الْقَمَرَ ۡ كُلٌّ
يَّجْرِيْٓ اِلٰٓى اَجَلٍ مُّسَمًّى وَّ اَنَّ اللّٰهَ بِمَا
تَعْمَلُوْنَ خَبِيْرٌ ﴿٢٩﴾

Thus it is, because Allah alone is the Ultimate Truth, so that all that men invoke instead of Him is sheer falsehood; and because Allah alone is exalted, truly great!

31:30

ذٰلِكَ بِاَنَّ اللّٰهَ هُوَ الْحَقُّ وَ اَنَّ مَا
يَدْعُوْنَ مِنْ دُوْنِهِ الْبٰطِلُ ۙ وَ اَنَّ اللّٰهَ
هُوَ الْعَلِيُّ الْكَبِيْرُ ﴿۳۰﴾ ع

Have they not observed what is
before them and what is behind
them of the sky and the earth? If We
will, We can make the earth swallow
them, or cause obliteration from the
sky to fall on them. Lo! herein surely is
a portent for every slave who turneth
(to Allah) repentant.

34:9

اَفَلَمْ يَرَوْا اِلٰى مَا بَيْنَ اَيْدِيْهِمْ وَمَا
خَلْفَهُمْ مِّنَ السَّمَآءِ وَالْاَرْضِ ؕ اِنْ
نَّشَاْ نَخْسِفْ بِهِمُ الْاَرْضَ اَوْ نُسْقِطْ
عَلَيْهِمْ كِسَفًا مِّنَ السَّمَآءِ ؕ اِنَّ فِيْ
ذٰلِكَ لَاٰيَةً لِّكُلِّ عَبْدٍ مُّنِيْبٍ ﴿٩﴾ ع

O men! Call to mind the grace of Allah unto you! is there a creator, other than Allah, to give you sustenance from heaven or earth? There is no god but He: how then are ye deluded away from the Truth.

35:3

يٰاَيُّهَا النَّاسُ اذْكُرُوْا نِعْمَتَ اللّٰهِ
عَلَيْكُمْ ؕ هَلْ مِنْ خَالِقٍ غَيْرُ اللّٰهِ
يَرْزُقُكُمْ مِّنَ السَّمَآءِ وَ الْاَرْضِ ؕ لَآ
اِلٰهَ اِلَّا هُوَ ۖ فَاَنّٰى تُؤْفَكُوْنَ ۝٣

And (know that) all of the Divine
Book (Quran) with which We
have inspired thee is the very truth,
confirming the truth of whatever there
still remains of earlier revelations for,
behold, of (the needs of) His servants
Allah is fully aware, all-seeing.

35:31

وَالَّذِيٓ اَوْحَيْنَآ اِلَيْكَ مِنَ الْكِتٰبِ
هُوَ الْحَقُّ مُصَدِّقًا لِّمَا بَيْنَ يَدَيْهِ ۭ اِنَّ
اللّٰهَ بِعِبَادِهٖ لَخَبِيْرٌۢ بَصِيْرٌ ﴿٣١﴾

And so, We have bestowed this Divine Book (Quran) as a heritage unto such of Our servants as We chose: and among them are some who sin against themselves; and some who keep half-way (between right and wrong); and some who, by Allah's leave, are foremost in deeds of goodness: (and) this, indeed, is a merit most high!

35:32

ثُمَّ اَوْرَثْنَا الْكِتٰبَ الَّذِيْنَ
اصْطَفَيْنَا مِنْ عِبَادِنَا ۚ فَمِنْهُمْ
ظَالِمٌ لِّنَفْسِهٖ ۚ وَ مِنْهُمْ مُّقْتَصِدٌ ۚ وَ
مِنْهُمْ سَابِقٌۢ بِالْخَيْرٰتِ بِاِذْنِ اللّٰهِ ؕ
ذٰلِكَ هُوَ الْفَضْلُ الْكَبِيْرُ ؕ ﴿٣٢﴾

If Allah took mankind to task by that which they deserve, He would not leave a living creature on the surface of the earth; but He reprieveth them unto an appointed term, and when their term cometh—then verily (they will know that) Allah is ever Seer of His slaves.

35:45

وَ لَوْ يُؤَاخِذُ اللّٰهُ النَّاسَ بِمَا
كَسَبُوْا مَا تَرَكَ عَلٰى ظَهْرِهَا مِنْ
دَآبَّةٍ وَّ لٰكِنْ يُّؤَخِّرُهُمْ اِلٰٓى اَجَلٍ
مُّسَمًّى ۚ فَاِذَا جَآءَ اَجَلُهُمْ فَاِنَّ اللّٰهَ
كَانَ بِعِبَادِهٖ بَصِيْرًا ﴿٤٥﴾ ع

It would not be reasonable in me if I did not serve Him Who created me, and to Whom you shall (all) be brought back.

36:22

وَمَا لِيَ لَآ اَعْبُدُ الَّذِيْ فَطَرَنِيْ وَاِلَيْهِ
تُرْجَعُوْنَ ﴿٢٢﴾

Surely, certainly, your Allah is one! Sustainer of the heavens and of the earth and all between them, and Sustainer of every point at the rising of the Sun!

37:4, 5

اِنَّ اِلٰـهَكُمْ لَوٰحِدٌ ؕ﴿۴﴾ رَبُّ السَّمٰوٰتِ
وَالْاَرْضِ وَمَا بَيْنَهُمَا وَرَبُّ
الْمَشٰرِقِ ؕ﴿۵﴾

For when it was said unto them (unbelievers), There is no god save Allah, they were scornful

37:35

إِنَّهُمْ كَانُوٓا إِذَا قِيلَ لَهُمْ لَآ إِلٰهَ إِلَّا
اللّٰهُ ۙ يَسْتَكْبِرُونَ ﴿٣٥﴾

Not thus, however, (behave) Allah's true servants. For, verily, neither ye nor those ye worship–Can lead (any) into temptation concerning Allah. Except such as are (themselves) going to the blazing Fire!

37:160–163

اِلَّا عِبَادَ اللّٰهِ الْمُخْلَصِيْنَ ﴿۱۶۰﴾
فَاِنَّكُمْ وَمَا تَعْبُدُوْنَ ﴿۱۶۱﴾ لا مَآ اَنْتُمْ
عَلَيْهِ بِفٰتِنِيْنَ ﴿۱۶۲﴾ لا اِلَّا مَنْ هُوَ صَالِ
الْجَحِيْمِ ﴿۱۶۳﴾ لا

Verily it is We Who have revealed the Book to thee in Truth: so serve Allah, offering Him sincere devotion.

39:2

إِنَّآ أَنْزَلْنَآ إِلَيْكَ الْكِتٰبَ بِالْحَقِّ

فَاعْبُدِ اللّٰهَ مُخْلِصًا لَّهُ الدِّيْنَ ؕ ﴿۲﴾

He has created you (all) out of one living entity, and out of it fashioned its mate; and he has bestowed upon you four kinds of cattle of either sex; (and) He creates you in your mothers' wombs, one act of creation after another, in threefold depths of darkness. Thus is Allah, your Sustainer: unto Him belongs all dominion: there is no deity save Him: how, then, can you lose sight of the truth?

39:6

خَلَقَكُمْ مِّنْ نَّفْسٍ وّٰحِدَةٍ
ثُمَّ جَعَلَ مِنْهَا زَوْجَهَا وَ اَنْزَلَ
لَكُمْ مِّنَ الْاَنْعٰمِ ثَمٰنِيَةَ اَزْوٰجٍ ط
يَخْلُقُكُمْ فِيْ بُطُوْنِ اُمَّهٰتِكُمْ خَلْقًا
مِّنْۢ بَعْدِ خَلْقٍ فِيْ ظُلُمٰتٍ ثَلٰثٍ ط
ذٰلِكُمُ اللّٰهُ رَبُّكُمْ لَهُ الْمُلْكُ ط لَآ
اِلٰهَ اِلَّا هُوَ ج فَاَنّٰى تُصْرَفُوْنَ ﴿٦﴾

If you are ingrate behold,
Allah has no need of you; none
the less, He does not approve of
ingratitude in His servants: whereas,
if you show gratitude, He approves it
in you. And no bearer of burdens shall
be made to bear another's burden. In
time, unto your Sustainer you all must
return, and then He will make you
(truly) understand all that you were
doing (in life): for, verily, He has full
knowledge of what is in the hearts
(of men).

39:7

اِنْ تَكْفُرُوْا فَاِنَّ اللّٰهَ غَنِيٌّ
عَنْكُمْ قف وَلَا يَرْضٰى لِعِبَادِهِ
الْكُفْرَ ج وَاِنْ تَشْكُرُوْا يَرْضَهُ
لَكُمْ ط وَلَا تَزِرُ وَازِرَةٌ وِّزْرَ
اُخْرٰى ط ثُمَّ اِلٰى رَبِّكُمْ مَّرْجِعُكُمْ
فَيُنَبِّئُكُمْ بِمَا كُنْتُمْ تَعْمَلُوْنَ ط
اِنَّهٗ عَلِيْمٌۢ بِذَاتِ الصُّدُوْرِ ﴿٧﴾

Say: Verily, I am commanded to serve Allah with sincere devotion; And I am commanded to be the first of those who bow to Allah in Islam.

39:11, 12

قُلْ اِنِّیْٓ اُمِرْتُ اَنْ اَعْبُدَ اللّٰهَ مُخْلِصًا
لَّهُ الدِّیْنَ ﴿۱۱﴾ وَ اُمِرْتُ لِاَنْ اَكُوْنَ اَوَّلَ
الْمُسْلِمِیْنَ ﴿۱۲﴾

Say: “Allah alone do I worship,
sincere in my faith in Him alone
and (it is up to you, O sinners, to)
worship whatever you please instead
of Him!” Say: “Behold, the (true) losers
will be they who shall have lost their
own selves and their kith and kin on
Resurrection Day: for is not this, this,
the (most) obvious loss?

39:14, 15

قُلِ اللّٰهَ اَعۡبُدُ مُخۡلِصًا لَّهٗ دِيۡنِىۡ ۙ ﴿١٤﴾
فَاعۡبُدُوۡا مَا شِئۡتُمۡ مِّنۡ دُوۡنِهٖ ؕ قُلۡ اِنَّ
الۡخٰسِرِيۡنَ الَّذِيۡنَ خَسِرُوۡۤا اَنۡفُسَهُمۡ وَ
اَهۡلِيۡهِمۡ يَوۡمَ الۡقِيٰمَةِ ؕ اَلَا ذٰلِكَ هُوَ
الۡخُسۡرَانُ الۡمُبِيۡنُ ﴿١٥﴾

It is Allah that takes the souls (of men) at death; and those that die not (He takes) during their sleep: those on whom He has passed the decree of death, He keeps back (from returning to life), but the rest He sends (to their bodies) for a term appointed verily in this are Signs for those who reflect.

39:42

اَللّٰهُ يَتَوَفَّى الْاَنْفُسَ حِيْنَ مَوْتِهَا وَ
الَّتِيْ لَمْ تَمُتْ فِيْ مَنَامِهَا ۚ فَيُمْسِكُ
الَّتِيْ قَضٰى عَلَيْهَا الْمَوْتَ وَ يُرْسِلُ
الْاُخْرٰۤى اِلٰۤى اَجَلٍ مُّسَمًّى ؕ اِنَّ فِيْ ذٰلِكَ
لَاٰيٰتٍ لِّقَوْمٍ يَّتَفَكَّرُوْنَ ﴿۴۲﴾

Say: "(Thus speaks Allah:) 'O you servants of Mine who have transgressed against your own selves! Despair not of Allah's mercy: behold, Allah forgives all sins–for, verily, He alone is much-forgiving, a dispenser of grace!'

39:53

قُلْ يٰعِبَادِیَ الَّذِیْنَ اَسْرَفُوْا عَلٰۤی
اَنْفُسِهِمْ لَا تَقْنَطُوْا مِنْ رَّحْمَةِ اللّٰهِ ط
اِنَّ اللّٰهَ یَغْفِرُ الذُّنُوْبَ جَمِیْعًا ط اِنَّهٗ
هُوَ الْغَفُوْرُ الرَّحِیْمُ ﴿۵۳﴾

And (so,) on the Day of Resurrection thou wilt see all who invented lies about Allah (with) their faces darkened (by grief and ignominy). Is not hell the (proper) abode for all who are given to false pride?

39:60

وَ يَوۡمَ الۡقِيٰمَةِ تَرَى الَّذِيۡنَ كَذَبُوۡا
عَلَى اللّٰهِ وُجُوۡهُهُمۡ مُّسۡوَدَّةٌ ؕ اَلَيۡسَ فِىۡ
جَهَنَّمَ مَثۡوًى لِّلۡمُتَكَبِّرِيۡنَ ﴿۶۰﴾

But Allah will safeguard all who were conscious of Him, (and will grant them happiness) by virtue of their (inner) triumphs; no evil shall ever touch them, and neither shall they grieve.

39:61

وَ يُنَجِّى اللّٰهُ الَّذِيْنَ اتَّقَوْا
بِمَفَازَتِهِمْ ۡ لَا يَمَسُّهُمُ السُّوْٓءُ وَلَا
هُمْ يَحْزَنُوْنَ ﴿٦١﴾

Say (O Muhammad, to the disbelievers): Do ye bid me to serve other than Allah? O you ignorant fools!

39:64

قُلْ اَفَغَيْرَ اللّٰهِ تَاْمُرُوْٓنِّيْٓ اَعْبُدُ اَيُّهَا
الْجٰهِلُوْنَ ﴿٦٤﴾

Nay, but Allah must thou serve, and be among the thankful!

39:66

بَلِ اللّٰهَ فَاعْبُدْ وَكُنْ مِّنَ الشّٰكِرِيْنَ ﴿٦٦﴾

Who forgives sin, accepts repentance, is strict in punishment, and has a long reach (in all things). There is no god but He: to Him is the final goal.

40:3

غَافِرِ الذَّنْۢبِ وَ قَابِلِ التَّوْبِ شَدِيْدِ
الْعِقَابِ ۙ ذِى الطَّوْلِ ؕ لَاۤ اِلٰهَ اِلَّا
هُوَ ؕ اِلَيْهِ الْمَصِيْرُ ۝٣

Say: “Since all evidence of the truth has come to me from my Sustainer, I am forbidden to worship (any of) those beings whom you invoke instead of Allah; and I am bidden to surrender myself to the Sustainer of all the worlds.”

40:66

قُلْ اِنِّیْ نُهِیْتُ اَنْ اَعْبُدَ الَّذِیْنَ
تَدْعُوْنَ مِنْ دُوْنِ اللّٰهِ لَمَّا جَآءَنِیَ
الْبَیِّنٰتُ مِنْ رَّبِّیْ ۡ وَاُمِرْتُ اَنْ اُسْلِمَ
لِرَبِّ الْعٰلَمِیْنَ ﴿٦٦﴾

Say to them (Muhammad), "I
am only a human being like you.
It has been Divinely revealed to me
that your God is one and the same;
the One and Only Allah. So, take the
straight path to Him and seek His
forgiveness. There is great loss for those
who choose Gods other than Him."

41:6

قُلْ اِنَّمَآ اَنَا بَشَرٌ مِّثْلُكُمْ يُوْحٰۤى اِلَيَّ
اَنَّمَآ اِلٰـهُكُمْ اِلٰهٌ وَّاحِدٌ فَاسْتَقِيْمُوْٓا
اِلَيْهِ وَاسْتَغْفِرُوْهُ ؕ وَوَيْلٌ
لِّلْمُشْرِكِيْنَ ۙ﴿۶﴾

His is all that is in the heavens and all that is on earth; and most exalted, tremendous is He.

42:4

لَهٗ مَا فِي السَّمٰوٰتِ وَمَا فِي الْاَرْضِ ؕ
وَهُوَ الْعَلِيُّ الْعَظِيْمُ ۝٤

So, it is to Him that we must always turn (for help and guidance).

43:14

وَ اِنَّآ اِلٰى رَبِّنَا لَمُنْقَلِبُوْنَ ﴿۱۴﴾

"Surely, Allah is my Sustainer as well as your Sustainer; so worship (none but) Him: this (alone) is a straight way!"

43:64

اِنَّ اللّٰهَ هُوَ رَبِّیۡ وَ رَبُّکُمۡ فَاعۡبُدُوۡہُ ؕ
هٰذَا صِرَاطٌ مُّسۡتَقِیۡمٌ ﴿۶۴﴾

It is He Who is Allah in heaven and Allah on earth; and He is full of Wisdom and Knowledge.

43:84

وَهُوَ الَّذِىْ فِى السَّمَآءِ اِلٰهٌ وَّفِى الْاَرْضِ
اِلٰهٌ ؕ وَهُوَ الْحَكِيْمُ الْعَلِيْمُ ﴿۸۴﴾

There is no supreme authority but He: It is He Who gives life and gives death,- The Sustainer and Cherisher to you and your earliest ancestors.

44:8

لَآ اِلٰهَ اِلَّا هُوَ يُحْيٖ وَ يُمِيْتُ ؕ رَبُّكُمْ
وَ رَبُّ اٰبَآئِكُمُ الْاَوَّلِيْنَ ﴿٨﴾

For (thus it is:) We have not created the heavens and the earth and all that is between them in mere idle play: none of this have We created without (an inner) truth but most of them understand it not.

44:38, 39

وَمَا خَلَقْنَا السَّمٰوٰتِ وَالْاَرْضَ
وَمَا بَيْنَهُمَا لٰعِبِيْنَ ﴿٣٨﴾ مَا خَلَقْنٰهُمَآ
اِلَّا بِالْحَقِّ وَلٰكِنَّ اَكْثَرَهُمْ لَا
يَعْلَمُوْنَ ﴿٣٩﴾

And do not ascribe divinity to anyone side by side with Allah certainly , I (Muhammad) am a plain warner to you from Him!

51:51

وَلَا تَجْعَلُوْا مَعَ اللّٰهِ اِلٰـهًا اٰخَرَ ؕ اِنِّىْ
لَكُمْ مِّنْهُ نَذِيْرٌ مُّبِيْنٌ ۚ ﴿٥١﴾

(Nay,) but prostrate yourselves before Allah, and worship (Him alone)

53:62

فَاسْجُدُوْا لِلّٰهِ وَ اعْبُدُوْا ﴿٦٢﴾ السجدة ع

And those who do not invoke any other god along with Allah, nor take the life which Allah has forbidden save in (course of) justice, nor commit adultery and whoso does this shall pay the penalty.

25:68

وَالَّذِيْنَ لَا يَدْعُوْنَ مَعَ اللّٰهِ اِلٰـهًا
اٰخَرَ وَ لَا يَقْتُلُوْنَ النَّفْسَ الَّتِيْ
حَرَّمَ اللّٰهُ اِلَّا بِالْحَقِّ وَ لَا يَزْنُوْنَ ۚ وَ
مَنْ يَّفْعَلْ ذٰلِكَ يَلْقَ اَثَامًا ﴿٦٨﴾ لا

Allah is He, than Whom there is no other god;–Who knows (all things) both secret and open; He, Most Gracious, Most Merciful.

59:22

هُوَ اللّٰهُ الَّذِىْ لَآ اِلٰهَ اِلَّا هُوَ ۚ عٰلِمُ
الْغَيْبِ وَ الشَّهٰدَةِ ۚ هُوَ الرَّحْمٰنُ
الرَّحِيْمُ ﴿٢٢﴾

Allah is He, than Whom there is no other god;–the Sovereign, the Holy One, the Source of Peace (and Perfection), the Guardian of Faith, the Preserver of Safety, the Exalted in Might, the Irresistible, the Supreme: Glory to Allah. (High is He) above the partners they attribute to Him.

59:23

هُوَ اللّٰهُ الَّذِیْ لَاۤ اِلٰهَ اِلَّا هُوَ ۚ اَلْمَلِكُ
الْقُدُّوْسُ السَّلٰمُ الْمُؤْمِنُ الْمُهَیْمِنُ
الْعَزِیْزُ الْجَبَّارُ الْمُتَكَبِّرُ ؕ سُبْحٰنَ
اللّٰهِ عَمَّا یُشْرِكُوْنَ ﴿۲۳﴾

He has created the heavens and the earth in accordance with (an inner) truth, and has formed you–and formed you so well; and to Him is your journey's end.

64:3

خَلَقَ السَّمٰوٰتِ وَ الْاَرْضَ بِالْحَقِّ وَ
صَوَّرَكُمْ فَاَحْسَنَ صُوَرَكُمْ ۚ وَ اِلَيْهِ
الْمَصِيْرُ ﴿٣﴾

Allah. There is no god but He: and in Allah, therefore, let the Believers put their trust.

64:13

اَللّٰهُ لَآ اِلٰهَ اِلَّا هُوَ ؕ وَعَلَى اللّٰهِ
فَلْيَتَوَكَّلِ الْمُؤْمِنُوْنَ ﴿١٣﴾

The Sustainer of the East and the West (is He): there is no deity save Him: hence, ascribe to Him alone the power to determine thy fate.

73:9

رَبُّ الْمَشْرِقِ وَ الْمَغْرِبِ لَآ اِلٰهَ اِلَّا
هُوَ فَاتَّخِذْهُ وَكِيْلًا ﴿٩﴾

Say: O disbelievers. I worship not that which ye worship and neither do you worship that which I worship. And I shall not worship that which ye worship. To you be your Way of life, and to me mine.

109:1–6

قُلْ يٰٓاَيُّهَا الْكٰفِرُوْنَ ۙ﴿۱﴾ لَآ اَعْبُدُ مَا
تَعْبُدُوْنَ ۙ﴿۲﴾ وَلَآ اَنْتُمْ عٰبِدُوْنَ مَآ
اَعْبُدُ ۚ﴿۳﴾ وَلَآ اَنَا عَابِدٌ مَّا عَبَدْتُّمْ ۙ﴿۴﴾
وَلَآ اَنْتُمْ عٰبِدُوْنَ مَآ اَعْبُدُ ؕ﴿۵﴾ لَكُمْ
دِيْنُكُمْ وَلِيَ دِيْنِ ﴿۶﴾ ع

SAY: He is the One Allah: Allah the Eternal, the Uncaused Cause of All Being. He begets not, and neither is He begotten; and there is nothing that could be compared with Him.

112:1–4

قُلْ هُوَ اللّٰهُ اَحَدٌ ۚ﴿١﴾ اَللّٰهُ الصَّمَدُ ۚ﴿٢﴾ لَمْ
يَلِدْ ۙ وَلَمْ يُوْلَدْ ۙ﴿٣﴾ وَلَمْ يَكُنْ لَّهٗ
كُفُوًا اَحَدٌ ﴿٤﴾ ع

Say: I seek refuge with the Sustainer of the rising dawn; From the mischief of created things; From the mischief of darkness as it overspreads; and from the evil of all human beings bent on occult endeavours, and from the evil of the envious when he envies

113:1–5

قُلْ اَعُوْذُ بِرَبِّ الْفَلَقِ ۙ﴿۱﴾ مِنْ شَرِّ مَا
خَلَقَ ۙ﴿۲﴾ وَ مِنْ شَرِّ غَاسِقٍ اِذَا وَقَبَ ۙ﴿۳﴾
وَ مِنْ شَرِّ النَّفّٰثٰتِ فِی الْعُقَدِ ۙ﴿۴﴾ وَ مِنْ
شَرِّ حَاسِدٍ اِذَا حَسَدَ ﴿۵﴾ ع

Say: I seek refuge with the Sustainer of mankind the Sovereign of mankind; The God of mankind; From the evil of the sneaking whisperer; who whispers in the hearts of men, from all (temptation to evil by) invisible forces as well as men.

114:1-6

قُلْ اَعُوْذُ بِرَبِّ النَّاسِ ۙ﴿۱﴾ مَلِكِ
النَّاسِ ۙ﴿۲﴾ اِلٰهِ النَّاسِ ۙ﴿۳﴾ مِنْ شَرِّ
الْوَسْوَاسِ ۙ۵ الْخَنَّاسِ ۙ﴿۴﴾ الَّذِیْ
یُوَسْوِسُ فِیْ صُدُوْرِ النَّاسِ ۙ﴿۵﴾ مِنَ
الْجِنَّةِ وَ النَّاسِ ﴿۶﴾ ع

ATTRIBUTES OF ALLAH

Allah	The Supreme Ruler, God's Proper Name
Ar-Rahman	The Beneficent
Ar-Raheem	The Merciful
Al-Malik	The Sovereign, The King Supreme
Al-Quddus	The Impeccable
As-Salam	The Source of Peace
Al-Mu'min	The Guardian of Tranquility
Al-Muhaimin	The Protector

Al-Aziz	The Almighty
Al-Jabbar	The One Who Carries All Things to Completion
Al-Mutakabbir	The Majestic
Al-Khaliq	The Creator
Al-Bari	The Creator from Nothing
Al-Musawwir	The Designer
Al-Ghaffar	The Forgiver
Ar-Razzaq	The Provider
Al-Fattah	The Opener of Gate to Victory
Al-'Aleem	The All-Knowing
Al-Basit	The Expander of Provision
Ar-Rafi'	The Exalter
Al-Mu'izz	The Honourer
As-Sami'	The All-Hearing
Al-Baseer	The All-Seeing
Al-Hakam	The Judge, The Ruler

Al-Lateef	The Subtle
Al-Khabeer	The Aware
Al-Haleem	The Clement
Al-'Azeem	The Magnificent
Al-Ghafoor	The All-Forgiving
Ash-Shakoor	The Appreciative
Al-'Aali	The Most High
Al-Akbar	The Greatest
Al-Hafeez	The Preserver
Al-Muqeet	The Maintainer
Ar-Rubb	The Sustainer
Al-Jaleel	The Sublime
Al-Kareem	The Generous
Ar-Raqeeb	The Watchful
Al-Mujeeb	The Responsive
Al-Waase'	The All-Embracing
Al-Hakeem	The Wise
Al-Wadud	The Loving
Al-Majeed	The Most Glorious
Ash-Shaheed	The Witness
Al-Haqq	The Truth

Al-Wakeel	The Guardian, The Defender
Al-Wali	The Protecting Friend
Al-Hameed	The Praiseworthy
Al-Badee'	The Originator
Al-Hayyi	The Eternally Alive
Al-Qayyum	The Self-subsisting Sustainer
Al-Ahad	The One
As-Samad	The Unique
Al-Qadir	The Able
Al-Awwal	The One With No Beginning
Al-Akhir	The One With No Ending
Ar-Ra'uf	The Compassionate
Al-Muqsit	The Equitable
Al-'Adil	The Just
Al-Qawi	The Most Strong
Al-Maalik	The Owner

Al-Ghani	The Self-Sufficient
An-Nur	The Universal Light
Al-Haadi	The Guide
Al-Baaqi	The Everlasting
Al-Mateen	The Firm
Al-Qahhaar	The Ultimate Decider, The Dominant
Al-Wahhaab	The Giver of Gifts